SENSUALITY
AND SEXUALITY
ACROSS THE
DIVIDE OF SHAME

Psychoanalytic Inquiry Book Series

Volume 25

Psychoanalytic Inquiry Book Series

SENSUALITY AND SEXUALITY ACROSS THE DIVIDE OF SHAME

Joseph D. Lichtenberg

The Analytic Press
Taylor & Francis Group

New York   London

The Analytic Press
Taylor & Francis Group
270 Madison Avenue
New York, NY 10016

The Analytic Press
Taylor & Francis Group
27 Church Road
Hove, East Sussex BN3 2FA

Printed in the United States of America on acid-free paper
10 9 8 7 6 5 4 3 2 1

International Standard Book Number-13: 978-0-88163-475-4 (Softcover) 978-0-88163-474-7 (Hardcover)

Library of Congress Cataloging-in-Publication Data

Lichtenberg, Joseph D.
   Sensuality and sexuality across the divide of shame / by Joseph D. Lichtenberg.
      p. ; cm. -- (Psychoanalytic inquiry book series ; v. 25)
   Includes bibliographical references and index.
   ISBN 978-0-88163-474-7 (alk. paper) -- ISBN 978-0-88163-475-4 (alk. paper)
   1. Psychoanalysis. 2. Sensuality. 3. Sex (Psychology) 4. Shame. I. Title. II. Series.
   [DNLM: 1. Psychoanalytic Theory. 2. Sexuality--psychology. 3. Interpersonal Relations. 4. Parent-Child Relations. 5. Shame. W1 PS427F v.25 2008 / WM 460.5.S3 L699s 2008]

   RC504.L53 2008
   616.89'17--dc22
                                                  2007017166

Visit the Taylor & Francis Web site at
http://www.taylorandfrancis.com

and The Analytic Press Web site at
http://www.analyticpress.com

*With attachment and love, I dedicate this book
to Charlotte, my wife, friend, and companion of nearly 60 years;
my wonderful children Ann, Amy, Maryland, and William;
their equally wonderful spouses Hank, Moustafa, Steve, and Vicky;
and my eight talented grandchildren
Katie, Andrew, and Lexie,
Jenny, Madalene, and Lizzy,
Allison and Lucas; and granddog Sedona.*

CONTENTS

ACKNOWLEDGMENTS

My idea to reconsider in depth my original presentation of the sensual–sexual motivational system began at the 2006 meeting of the Eastern Division of the International Association for Psychoanalytic Self Psychology (IAPSP) in Boston. I was stimulated by a presentation of Malcolm Slavin and discussions by all the members but particularly Shelley Doctors and my prior coauthors Frank Lachmann and James Fosshage. My already-formed central conception about the role of culture-derived shame separating sensuality and sexuality crystallized as I heard Peter Fonagy present a similar proposal using a different frame to develop it. As I wrote different chapters, I was aided and stimulated by discussions by numerous colleagues at presentations, such as at the 2006 IAPSP meeting in Chicago. I am especially indebted to Adrienne Harris, Estelle Shane, Sandra Hershberg, Heidi Block, and Andrew Morrison, who have led me to make specific additions and reformulations. Alan Kindler introduced me to the research of Katherine Frank and provided me with the opportunity to present chapters 1 and 2 to the Toronto Association for Self Psychology. My colleagues in an Institute of Contemporary Psychotherapy and Psychoanalysis study group chaired by Curtis Bristol have been generous and dedicated in their chapter-by-chapter discussion. I have borrowed (maybe shamelessly) from other sources to which I have had unique access: the Psychoanalytic Inquiry issues on Mothers and Daughters edited by Rosemary Balsam and Ruth Fischer, the Issue on Fathers and Daughters edited by Christine Kiefer, and the book *Attachment and Sexuality* edited by Diana Diamond, Sidney Blatt, and me. Elisabeth Fivaz-Depeursinge kindly invited me to view research tapes of her studies of family triangles in Lausanne, Switzerland, findings to which I have referred frequently. Paul Stepansky, the former head of The Analytic Press, has consistently encouraged my efforts. Many of the perspectives to which I refer in the text derive from friends and colleagues, like that of Robert Stolorow on intersubjectivity, Jessica Benjamin on subjectivity in female development, Steven Mitchell and Lewis Aron on the relational perspective, and Ernest Wolf on selfobject experience. These approaches have become a core way of my thinking. My daughter, Amy Lichtenberg Saloukha, was instrumental in the preparation of the manuscript. My wife, Charlotte, patiently read and listened to portions of the manuscript, especially those for which I had uncertainties, and offered her sage advice. Finally, for me as a psychoanalyst, the most meaningful testing ground for proposals like those I advance is in the clinical setting of my patients and me struggling to come as close to getting it "right" about their and my sensual and sexual experiences as it affects their happiness and ability to relate, love, and lust lovingly. My final debt is to the many men and women who have trustingly revealed their inner and usually private worlds to me.

INTRODUCTION

Sex, according to an anonymous wit, is the joker in the deck. Looking at most recent mainstream psychoanalytic literature, a reader could easily conclude sex, rather than any longer a wild card, has been tamed into established formulas such as psychosexual stages and an Oedipus complex. *New Yorker* cartoons attest to the public familiarity with and acceptance of these abstractions. Fonagy (2006), in his plenary address on a genuinely developmental theory of sexual enjoyment, noted: "A frightening survey of the use of sexual and relational language in the electronically searchable journals of psychoanalysis showed a dramatic decline in words in psychoanalytic articles directly concerning sexuality." In 1996 (pp. 871–883), Green asked sardonically, "Has sexuality anything to do with psychoanalysis?" Of course, there are exceptions. A considerable body of literature has been developed by feminists and by analysts reconsidering formulations about homosexuality. In 2000, a journal, *Studies in Gender and Sexuality,* began publication. Mitchell in 2002 wrote *Can Love Last? The Fate of Romance Over Time.* Another exception that I draw on extensively is the contribution made by analytic researchers steeped in attachment theory to sexuality (Diamond, Blatt, & Lichtenberg, 2007).

My hope is to draw the reader back to a consideration of sex as a wild card through a reformulation of the distinction between sensuality and sexuality. In each reformulation, I start with phenomena such as general observations and clinical vignettes. Obviously, all psychoanalytic formulations started with phenomena, such as symptoms, but the criticism of phenomenology has been that observables do not reveal unconscious processes—only psychoanalytically obtained information does. I agree with this critique, but I am not deterred by it. After over half a century as a psychoanalytic clinician, I believe that I can combine the two sources. Put more strongly, I believe I cannot *not* combine a phenomenological and analytic approach because that is how I think. Here, I reach back to observable phenomena as a starting point to disentangle existing theory to take a fresh look at sensuality and sexuality.

My main contribution (developed in chapter 1) is simple but, if accepted, is far reaching. All infants, toddlers, and older children seek pleasurable body sensations and schemas and fantasies that elaborate hedonic bodily experience, and all parents and other authorities respond to children's pleasure sensation seeking either by approving, sharing, and encouraging or by disapproving, shaming, and prohibiting. From that easily observable phenomenon of discrepant culture-driven responses, I make a small leap. The approved of, shared in, and encouraged forms of pleasurable body sensations and accompanying fantasies I refer to as *sensuality*. Sensual exchanges contribute to a broad spectrum of shared human experiences, from deep attachments, to friendships, to pleasant moments with self, others, and pets. The disapproved of, shamed, and prohibited forms of pleasurable body sensations and accompanying fantasies I refer to as *sexuality*. I argue that, from its inception in the anxious culture-determined turning away and shaming by parents in response to particular children's pleasure-seeking desires, sexuality takes a path toward excitement that builds from both a hedonic quest and a response to transgressing the shaming and prohibiting. Taking off from both pleasure/excitement seeking and breaking through prohibitions and prohibitors, sexuality becomes the joker in the deck by including in its expression subversive and transgressive aspects. My claim of the significance of the experiential disparity between sensuality and sexuality (in both their formal expressions and conscious and unconscious fantasy elaboration) is described throughout the book as it applies to dyadic and triadic experiences and to romantic love throughout life.

In prior books (Lichtenberg, 1989; Lichtenberg, Lachmann, & Fosshage, 1992), I developed a theme of five motivational systems, one of which is the sensual–sexual system. In these presentations, the interplay of competing systems is described in detail. Each may be dominant at any moment, the others subsidiary or latent. In this book, I primarily focus on sensuality and sexuality and the particular relationship to the attachment–affiliative motivational system. The other systems enter the discussion without a formal consideration of the interrelationships.

The reader may encounter a problem in using the terms sensuality and sexuality as I describe and define their usage in my theoretical claim. I am placing much weight and meaning on two descriptors—sensuality and sexuality—that already have preexisting meanings in a reader's mind. I hope my phenomenological examples succeed in evoking the kind of examples in the reader's own experience to carry the weight of my argument about the different paths taken by sensuality and sexuality.

A word is needed on what I include and what I omit. Sensuality and sexuality are vast subjects, ranging from a mother and a baby's first experience of sucking to the permutations of romantic love and lust in adult life. I have chosen to write about only areas in which I believe I have something to add to existing theory and areas in which I have had sufficient personal experience as observer and clinical participant to have confidence in my inferences. Essentially, I build off my background in classical theory, ego psychology, self-psychology, the relational perspective, infant research, attachment theory, my contributions to motivational systems theory, and my knowledge of sociocultural influences. Although this includes a lot, much also remains outside the domain over which I feel I can claim any mastery. My hope is that the reader will find enough intriguing perspectives in what I offer to compensate for the areas of omission.

CHAPTER 1

Looking at Sensuality and Sexuality Across the Divide of Shame

INTRODUCTION

Contemporary revisions in self-psychology, relational, and other psychoanalytic theories leave analysts with the question: If sexuality is not the product of a sexual drive, then what is it? The question can best be approached by observing infants and caretakers and conjecturing on the embodied minds of each as they engage in specific interplay. This exploration revisits the sensual–sexual motivational system (Lichtenberg, 1989) with a greater appreciation of the developmental role of intersubjectivity. I emphasize the central role of shame in distinguishing what comes to be experienced as either sensuality or sexuality. My inquiry begins with an appreciation of an infant and developing child's body sensation pleasure interacting with cultural values mediated by caregivers who indicate sanctioned forms through approval and unsanctioned forms through shaming. I suggest that transgressing into unsanctioned forms of body pleasure and fantasy becomes a universal component of sexuality. The interplay between desire and prohibition creates an experience of tension in sexuality not present in sensuality. Whether an individual's form of sexual expression follows or deviates from practices acceptable to that individual's society is important to the degree and quality of shame and guilt that person has to bear. Likewise, an analyst's tolerance or revulsion in response to an analysand's forms of sexual expression will influence the treatment, as I indicate from my clinical experience.

When she gave birth to her first child, my daughter requested that I be in the delivery room with her and her husband to back them up on maintaining their breathing exercise. After the delivery, the obstetrician handed the baby to the nurse, who plunked the crying neonate on the medication table. After administering to her, the nurse handed her to me, and in my cradling arms her loud "protest" crying reduced to a whimper. I placed her on her mother's chest, and the whimpering stopped as soon as the baby heard her mother's heartbeat. I asked my daughter if she would like to try to initiate a feeding. I knew that no breast milk would be available 5 minutes after birth, but it would serve as priming for the first feeding. My daughter agreed and asked me to position the baby. I put the baby's head near the nipple and chucked her cheek to elicit rooting. The baby turned her head, clasped onto the nipple with her mouth, and began to suck. A beautiful smile came over the mother's face that was shared immediately by me and other onlookers.

This vignette is a story of multiple levels of attachment: a newborn baby to her mother and her mother to her; my daughter to her husband and her husband to her and their baby; my daughter to me and me to my daughter, her husband, and their baby. It could also be described as a continuation of the baby's intrauterine attachment based on her familiarity with her mother's heartbeat. The vignette is also a story of the beginning of physiological regulation of feeding as a priming episode and the beginning of the capacity for self-righting from an aversive state (crying) to a calm state. My principal reason for relating this cherished memory is to delineate the powerful presence of sensuality. A small example occurred the moment the nurse handed the baby to me and I lovingly nestled her into my arms. This was certainly a sensual moment for me as I felt the baby's skin and possibly for the baby as she shifted from crying to whimpering. Then, with skin-to-skin contact with her mother, a definitely sensual moment emerged for each of them. The level of sensual enjoyment of tactile stimulation was further increased for the baby through nonnutritive sucking and for the mother through the stimulation of her nipple and areola.

A second example of shared sensuality also involves breast-feeding. Sammy, an infant observed in a study, at 3 months and his mother have established a comfortable feeding rhythm. As he sucks, his little fist against her breast slowly opens, and with his small fingers he strokes her soft skin. Experiencing the pleasurable tactile sensations, she looks down lovingly at him as they jointly enjoy the sensuality. Her affectionate glance down may be a tiny bit quizzical if she felt aroused by an implicit or explicit association to fondling or feeling "felt up."

Now, move ahead to Sammy at 3½. His mother allows him to climb up next to her as she breast-feeds his baby sister. Calming from his initial fussing at exclusion, Sammy begins to look with fascination at the sucking baby and his mother's breast. Sammy starts to reach for her breast, and his mother rebukes him, saying: "No. No. Sammy you mustn't." His interest-excitement inhibited, Sammy looks downcast and crushed before he begins to protest again.

In both of the observations, Sammy is drawn to the tactile pleasure of touching his mother's breast. In the first instance, his touch is welcomed by a mirroring glance of his mother, who is pleased and happy to share their rising pleasurable exchange. I suggest it is as if she were saying to him: "Sammy you are a sensual little boy, and I am a sensual woman, and together we can enjoy sensuality without shame or maybe with just the tiniest hint of embarrassment on my part." In the second observation, a similar interest in tactile pleasure is no longer responded to with pleasurable acceptance and sharing. As with most experiences, the motives are complex. Sammy's initial fuss is anger and envy at his mother shutting out and replacing him, and his mother tries to respond by offering him inclusion. The component of the experience I am centering on is Sammy's hand reaching to touch his mother's breast. The motivation behind his gesture includes having what his sister has, but mainly, I believe, he is reactivating a somatic memory of a pleasurable sensual experience repeated many times over before his weaning.

So, what has changed? Probably outside of her awareness, Sammy's mother is influenced by two different value systems prescribed by her culture. One evaluation concludes the young baby's touching, exploring, and fondling are innocent of intentions regarded as naughty, dirty, or even perverse. Innocent intentions to arouse pleasurable body–mind experiences, intentions I refer to as *sensual*, are not regarded by Sammy's mother as threats to excite her or Sammy. She does not attribute to herself or Sammy an intrusion of lustful desire into their personal Garden of Eden so celebrated in portrayals of Madonna and child.

Sammy's mother uses a different value system to evaluate the actions and intentions of the 3½-year-old, who she sees as wanting to play with her breast, demarcated at this point as a sexual body part. Collateral annoyance at Sammy for interfering with the ongoing feeding may have accentuated her irritability but is not central to the message: "You may not fondle my breast." More precisely, the message was: "Curb your excitement, curb that kind of action and the arousal it aims for and will generate. Your intention, if not impeded, will lead to actions and excitement that are shameful. You, and we, will have crossed the line that divides what is 'innocent', acceptable, containable, affectionate sensuality from what is unacceptable, dangerously arousing, lustful sexuality."

Shameful is a moral or ethical evaluation of an action and the actor. *Shame* is an emotion that has the effect of blunting initiative and curbing interest-excitement. Shame is also an emotion that may be activated when, for whatever reason, initiative is blunted and interest-excitement is curbed. Sammy has his interest and arousal suddenly curbed by his mother's prohibition that signals bad action, bad intention, bad boy. Once shamed, Sammy casts his eyes down, his body posture slumps, and his lips turn down at the sides. He does not remain long in a shame state but moves into an irritable sulk. Climbing off the chair that holds his mother and sister, he begins to throw his toys. This brings on another, now-angry, admonition from mother for him to stop. "Bad boy" now combines sexual badness (actually a gentle movement of his arm to fondle the breast) with angry destructive badness (the more violent movement of his arms throwing his toys). In Sammy's lived experience, the relatively straightforward "innocent" sensually motivated gesture is converted first into a mildly conflictual "naughty" sexual desire through mother's shaming restraint and second through the subsequent temper protest and mother's intensified shaming prohibition into a conflict over willfulness.

To summarize, sensuality involves a pleasurable body sensation shared with another who looks on (mirrors) the activity benignly as participant or witness. Sensuality may also involve a pleasurable body sensation when alone, accompanied by an afterimage of a mirroring other implicitly conveying approval. Sensuality originates as body-generated experiences in the presymbolic period. Once symbolic processing begins, body-generated experiences can activate imagination, fantasies, and dream imagery. Imagination, fantasy, and dream imagery can activate or intensify body-generated sensual experiences.

Sexuality involves a pleasurable body sensation that, when sought, is interrupted by a prohibiting response. For a developing child or adolescent, sexuality is a "package" that combines a desire based on memory of a prior pleasurable sensation or an immediate body sensation urge (itch) and an authority who, rather than mirror, share, and comfortably regulate the flow of the urge, prohibits its fulfillment. The view stated here is similar in some regard to Fonagy's depiction of the affirming effect of mirroring and the contrasting effect of its absence in establishing sexuality as "alien"(Fonagy, 2006). As with sensuality, sexual desire can originate from two sources. The prohibited body-generated experiences can activate imagination, fantasies, and dream imagery. Alternatively, imagination, fantasy, and dream imagery can activate or intensify prohibited body-generated sexual experiences.

To understand the role of shame as a critical element in this package requires an examination of shame as a primary regulator-inhibitor of interest-excitement.

THE ROLE OF SHAME AS REGULATOR-INHIBITOR

Tomkins (1987) regarded shame as an innate affect present in early infancy. In Tomkins's view, shame becomes activated when a barrier to an ongoing experience of interest-excitement or excitement-joy dampens, but does not eliminate, the interest or enjoyment. If Tomkins's hypothesis of the triggering effect of interrupted interest and enjoyment is correct and shame is an innate response present at birth, then shame must be frequently experienced by preverbal children. As each motivational system becomes activated, as each intention mounts, interest is triggered. In many situations, varying degrees of excitement and joy follow, sometimes generated principally by the infant's own activity, more often by the added participation and encouragement of a caregiver. A parent's active participation in feeding, social contact, toy play, or rocking will support the infant's interest. Further, a mother or father's indications of approval of touching, fondling, sucking, or cuddling with blankets and soft toys will enhance the child's sensual experience and vitalize a feeling state. But, often parents need to interrupt a feeding, social contact, toy play, or rocking to take care of another of the baby's needs or of a need of their own. When an activity is interrupted, infants can easily be observed having an aversive response. Some infants evidence anger and thrashing about in efforts to resume the activity. Many infants evidence a postural change, slumping body, lowered eyes, or averted gaze that may be experienced as the affect of shame or shame-sadness.

In contrast to Tomkins (1987), Lewis (1992) argued that shame begins as an affective response of verbal children (aged 18–24 months) who can recognize their caregiver's view of them and then view themselves similarly. "Success or failure in regard to abiding by standards, rules, and goals provides a signal to the self. This signal affects the organism and allows individuals to reflect upon themselves. This reflection is made on the basis of self-evaluation. The self-attribution one makes determines the nature of the resulting emotion" (p. 66).

Integrating Tomkins (1987) and Lewis (1992), I propose the following schema for shame as a preverbal and verbal contributor to the divide between sensuality and sexuality:

1. Shame as an affective, nonreflective, non-self-attributive experience frequently occurs in the daily lives of infants and young toddlers. Shame as a reflective self-attributive experience frequently occurs in the daily lives of older children and adults.
2. Caregivers often interrupt an infant's rising interest in sucking his or her fingers, mushing their food, touching and fondling their genitals, and playing with their feces and thus automatically trigger an affect that many times may be experienced as shame.
3. Caregiver's choice of what body pleasure seeking to encourage and what to inhibit is often an expression of procedural memory. In this way, caregivers introduce a " ghost in the nursery"—their own infant lived experience. Thus, parent–child interactions reflect a transgenerational influence and the

impact of culture on what is acceptable (= sensual) and what is to be censored (= sexual).

4. Shame, especially acting as a regulatory signal, is an important contributor to the socializing and acculturating of infants and toddlers during the period when the sense of self is forming.

5. Whether shame as a lived experience makes an adaptive contribution to a relatively flexible regulation of undesired body pleasure-seeking behaviors or results in pathological inhibitions and a lowered sense of self-worth will be determined by the vulnerability of the child's temperament and the frequency, severity, and empathic or unempathic manner with which caregivers activate shame and the length of time infants are allowed or required to remain in a shame state before reparative efforts occur.

6. Sexuality carries with its emergence an inevitable quality of conflict and tension between "I want to" and "I must not." To carry forward with "I want to," the child, adolescent, or adult must assert varying degrees of agency, ranging from mild defiance to angry transgressive determination.

7. An affirmation–shame balance may be generalized from the lived experiences of the preverbal period and will influence fundamental nonconscious and conscious mentation and the quality and form of symbolization of both sensuality and sexuality.

8. At any time during life, an established affirmation–shame balance may be pathologically disturbed if caregivers, peers, teachers, or strangers exploit the infant's, child's, adolescent's, or adult's body for their transgressive aggressive desires.

9. In this schema, I understate the dyadic, bidirectional nature of the relationship between caregivers and infants. Infants, especially toddlers, are lively contributors to the interplay between prohibition-shame and the retention, intensity, and persistence of the desire for bodily pleasure. The outcome, that is, the qualities of sexuality, are coconstructed by child and mother, child and father, and child and mother and father, all within the context of a particular culture. Likewise, the involvement of other caretakers and siblings sought by the child or seeking the child with their sexual needs and values may be significant.

10. I also understate the unpredictability of any single or repeated prohibition and of any self- or interactive attempt at regulation. As symbolic play and verbal communication come into play after 18 months, the self-attributive nature of shame adds further unpredictability through the ambiguity of inference making and imagination. A prohibition may be elaborated in

fantasy as far more or less threatening than intended. The violation of a prohibition against masturbating or voyeurism may evoke combinations of shame, guilt, shyness, fear, or anger or, alternatively, satisfaction, pride, and defiance.

11. I also neglect to describe explicitly the impact on selfobject experience of my conception of sensuality and sexuality. Sensuality easily originates from the sharing of selfobject experiences of pleasant bodily and aesthetically arousing experiences that vitalize or soothe as needs for each arise. Sexuality is more complex. Shaming and the arousal of other related aversive affects means the temporary loss of a feeling of self-worth following Morrison's (1989) felicitous phrase that shame is the underside of narcissism. In a generally empathic setting, the person easily recovers from narcissistic injury, and the acculturation provides a useful guide. When admonishments and prohibitions are delivered without sensitivity to the child's subjectivity, roots are planted for difficulties for later selfobject experiences to emerge from sexual expression. However, even a basically positive selfobject experience during sexual activity does not mean that sexuality can ever escape a degree of tension related to prohibition and the transgressive nature inherent in sexual expression.

Freud's (1924) linked the Oedipus complex and a desire for genital excitement with its prohibition (see chapter 2). The prohibition was based on three sources: an incest taboo, the opposition of the opposite sex parent, and the immaturity of the child. Considering the tragic frequency of trauma from sexual exploitation of children by parents, siblings, and parental surrogates (babysitters, priests, teachers), we can no longer accept Freud's belief in the universal power of an incest taboo prohibition through the overpowering guilt it engenders. Fear of retaliation from the rival parent, symbolized as castration or body damage anxiety, is a factor, but so is respect for the parental relationship and shame at the child's inclination to rid him- or herself of a loving and supportive mother or father. An additional source of inhibition arises from the shame and embarrassment children experience from the immaturity of their general body-mind and genitals and the limitations of their ability to perform when confronted by the mysteries and goals of adult sexuality. This source of narcissistic injury, genital inferiority, and performance anxiety must be overcome in adolescence and the early adult years.

Beginning at age 5, and increasingly by age 9, children can express in words the features they associate with shame and guilt (Ferguson,

Stegge, & Damhuis, 1991). Feelings of guilt are aroused by moral norm violations and are associated with remorse, a desire to make amends, and fear of punishment. Feelings of shame are described as resulting from both moral transgressions and social blunders. Younger children associate shame with embarrassment, blushing, ridicule, and a desire to escape. Young teens also characterize shame as feeling stupid (not knowing the "facts of life"), incapability of doing things right (wearing the right clothes, making the right "moves"), and feeling too shy to look at or approach opposite sex children.

Although I am implicating shame as the principal affect that the pre-verbal and verbal child experiences in response to the prohibition of his or her body pleasure seeking, shame is often experienced in conjunction with other negative affects, such as shame-fear, shame-anger, or shame-sadness. Embarrassment, humiliation, guilt, and shyness are shame-related affective experiences. All these varied affects may be associated with an initial prohibition, a reactivation of the desire, a suppression of the desire, or a transgressive break through of the desire into a sexual expression.

THE BOUNDARIES OF THE DOMAIN
OF SENSUAL AND SEXUAL EXPERIENCE

When sensual body pleasure in infancy and childhood is mirrored approvingly, sensual interest and satisfaction are easily integrated with motivations that are not based in body sensation pleasure. The interest-excitement triggered by the sensual pleasure of viewing an affirming smiling face and the vocal tonalities of affectionate caregivers provides a precursor for the sensual pleasure of viewing nature and art and listening to music. The cross-modal perception and integration of one sensory modality (touch, sight, sound, taste, or smell) opens the way for experiences of sensual pleasure to cross all perceptual modes. Rhythms of sensuality can range from slow soporific rocking to a lullaby while clutching an odor-filled blanket to the fast pace of a swing and a hand clapping a patterned song. All this blends easily into attachment experiences and contributes greatly to a sense of intimacy with others and self.

Shame, the innate affect activated when an ongoing experience of pleasure in body sensations is inhibited, as I noted becomes modified into more differentiated affects and situational patterns. The refusal by a mother of her child's effort to gain affection or the refusal of a father to allow his child to sit on his lap can evoke a temporary feeling of humiliation and, if repeated often, a feeling of discouragement. A child or adult expecting to be regarded as attractive in a shared mirroring gaze may instead be regarded with a cold stare of objectifying appraisal or the hot ogling of a sexually exploitative other. These responses evoke blushing and embarrassment. Uncertainty about how an overture for a desire will be received will often trigger shyness and reticence.

In each situation of regulation-inhibition by shame, humiliation, discouragement, embarrassment, or shyness, a child is confronted with the need to push against or find a way around the barrier to fulfill the unextinguished sexual urge. Direct attack on the prohibition involves feeling demanding, rebellious, and defiant. Indirect attack involves secretiveness and additional shame. Guilt is evoked by a direct attack against or injury to a loved caregiver or an indirect attack or rebellion against an accepted moral principle.

The view I have presented thus far can be regarded as a "clean" or idealized version of the development of sensuality and sexuality across the divide of shame. Caregivers are often not gentle and empathic in their prohibitions. Procedural memory can lead a mother to yank her son's thumb out of his mouth or smack her daughter hard for genital fondling. Procedural memory can lead a father to slam the door in the face of a child peaking at him to see his genitals. Cuddling, holding, and rocking can be so restricted lest the child be "spoiled" that sensuality shrinks to a body drained of pleasurable sensations without a breakthrough of intense sexual excitement.

In considering the spread of boundaries of sexuality, children find that roughhousing and mild pain enhance body pleasure sensations. Teasing, tickling, nibbling, biting, pinching, and chasing have mixtures of erotic arousal augmented by discomfort. Moreover, a child's natural interest in touching, smelling, or mushing his food, feces, or any gelatinous substance may invoke not a "You must not," but a response that not only stigmatizes the action but also debases the doer as dirty, revolting, and rotten to the core. This Eew! or Ick! factor (Dimen, 2005) of severely inhibiting humiliation, shame, and disgust and of loathsomeness in one's desire and practices is the counterpoint to the contempt, disdain, and righteous indignation of the prohibitor.

THE CLINICAL CHALLENGE OF THE ANALYST'S REVULSION AT THE PATIENT'S EXPRESSION OF SEXUALITY

An analyst's reactions of revulsion—the Eew! factor—can create a difficult challenge for the analysis. Generally, patients who bring to the analysis their severe problematic inhibitions based on parental disgust or other traumatic experiences will evoke supportive efforts by the analyst to overcome the paralysis of the patient's initiative to achieve sexual interest, excitement, and orgastic release; that is, this will occur unless the analyst shares the revulsion. An analyst's reaction of disgust-revulsion or startle-revulsion when triggered by the particular sexual practices adopted by patients in their effort to break free of problematic inhibitions challenges the analyst to examine his or her own Eew! factor.

I describe five clinical vignettes in which my response to the patient led to an enactment comparable to that of a parent's revulsion-shaming-prohibition. As with any other intense emotional expression, the Eew! factor can take on different forms. One form is the nose turned up, wrinkled brow, upturned lip response to a smelly diaper with a eew sound. This form is based on a primitive reaction of dyssmell (Tomkins, 1962, 1963). Another form is eyebrows turned up, eyes wide, mouth open with the verbal utterance, "What! What *are* you doing?" This form is based on the more cognitive appraisal of the breach of some standard such as a mother's discovery of two children having taken off their clothes and playing with each other's genitals. I refer to the first form as *disgust-revulsion* and the second as *startle-revulsion*. Both forms result in shaming, humiliating, and embarrassing the recipient and stopping an ongoing pleasurable and exciting action or fantasy in its tracks. The examples I present can be regarded as a challenge for me to recover my equilibrium sufficiently for me to regain an empathic mode of perception (a problem of self-regulation). In addition, the examples can be regarded as an opportunity through the enactment to work with and explore the patient's sexual patterns that evoked my revulsion (mutual regulation). Although my disgust or shock response was analogous to the original parental shame–prohibition response, neither the source as a sexual practice nor the form of response was identical. The analogy of pleasure–excitement seeker and repulsed–prohibitor relationship was sufficiently close to open the issue for an important relational struggle at a relatively primitive intense level and to make explicit inquiry into the patients' often-desperate need to find an avenue for closeness and a sexual outlet for passion. To open the issue for a mutual regulation in exploration, I had to carry in my mind both the patient's sexual behavior that I found repulsive and the person whose basic desire for aliveness and connection I could empathically sense and relate to sympathetically.

Sister Mary (Lichtenberg, 2000, 2005, pp. 109–113, 115, 126) was adviser to a young adult considering joining the order to which she belonged. The young woman, Grace, became attached and dependent. With a mixture of defiance and shame, Sister Mary revealed that they embraced often and fondled one another. Included in my attempts to understand and interpret Sister Mary's motivation were expressions of my concern about appearances and exposure. Sister Mary was generally so rebellious about rules that my concerns about risk went unappreciated and unheeded. She reported in a glow that she had had a wonderful weekend. Grace had visited and agreed to stay overnight. They undressed and fondled all over and satisfied themselves lovingly. In a voice that revealed my mixture of disapproval, concern, and alarm, I said she was involving herself sexually against her own commitment as a spiritual adviser. Even more of a problem, she was sexually enticing a young woman who had placed trust in her. She became outraged, telling me that everything I said was further proof of my dirty mind. She insisted that their embracing was an expression of love. It provided her with a badly needed affirmation that she was worthy of love, and that another woman was appreciating her large body, so depreciated by her mother. She roared: "This was love, not sex!" Without reflection, I roared back: "When you and another person get in bed naked and masturbate one another, that is sex! Whatever else is involved, it is sex!" A silence followed that seemed an expression of exhaustion after the intensity of emotion and a restoration of reflection on both our parts as we regained our composure. What followed was unexpected. Sister Mary explained to Grace that they could not continue; it was not good for either. Grace needed to look elsewhere for a loving relationship (which she subsequently did).

In the analysis of Mary Jane (Lichtenberg, 2005, pp. 49–50, 92–94, 96), I met the challenge of revulsion with more equanimity. Mary Jane, a divorced professor, had typical borderline problems with regulation across the entire spectrum of motivational systems. She had been emotionally abused by both parents and as a young teen sexually seduced by a priest who was her father's best friend. She also remembered as a 3-year-old having been held down, kicking and screaming, as a catheter was inserted. Desperate as an adolescent for affection and affirmation, she had been provocative and promiscuous. Again desperate after her divorce, she used the Internet to invite contact with men and frequently used telephone sex as a presleep excitement-release-soporific. She announced that she was going to Europe to meet Sven, an understanding physician with whom she had been having telephone sex and long Internet and phone conversations. She asked if I had read a book she had given me from Sex and Love Addicts Anonymous on addiction. I answered yes, and she replied that then she could tell me what she was planning. She handed me a picture of a woman's body bound in bondage with needles in her breasts and looked at me apprehensively as she explained that Sven shared her interest in this sexual enactment and agreed to get the necessary equipment.

My reaction was startle-revulsion. What awful sexual sadomasochistic craziness was she getting into now? Moving from revulsion to more amazement, my initial repugnance faded. I believe I took inspiration from

Robert Stoller's (1975) nonjudgmental interest in people (not patients as such) with unusual sexual practices. I began to inquire about her plan, and during the next several sessions, she described how important this sharing of a sexual interest with an understanding man was to her. She thought of it as a breakthrough experience in which a man would do something to her body that would hurt just right—not too much, but just right. She was certain that, under her direction, he would ever so carefully insert the needles, and the experience would be ecstatic. I came to understand this sadomasochistic practice as one in which, rather than ceding power to the dominator, Mary Jane shared the power as codirector of the action, a reversal of her childhood position of having been held, screaming, as she was catheterized and her young teen position with the seducer priest and her disbelieving, rejecting family.

The challenge of the Eew! factor took on a different form with Rob, a young, gay businessman. I was fond of Rob, who worked hard in treatment. He reported frequent sex with partners, usually anal penetration with the positions shifting. He also at times sought out anonymous sex. We made little effort to explore his choice of sexual practice, mainly concentrating on his attachment longings and the problems of growing up gay in his family. He reported a dream in which a clear stand-in for me was identified as a fist fucker. To my inquiry, he explained a fist fucker was a man who jammed his fist up his partner's ass. I was both stunned and revolted to picture myself cast in this image. My Eew! factor was primarily in response to portrayal with such assaultive aggression, not, I believe, to anal entry between men. Rob's associations shed no light on the meaning of the dream, and nothing more was said about it in subsequent sessions. However, I puzzled over the lingering image.

Rob, now in a committed relationship, entered an ending phase of treatment. For the first time, he explicitly raised the subject of my attitude about gays—prejudiced, he assumed like his father's. I was compelled by the forthright honesty of the attribution to consider it from multiple angles. One angle was my memory of teenage affection-longing for my best friend; another was my going along as a young adult with an ambiguous invitation to attend a party with a group of artists and performers that I "knew," despite denial, were gay; another was my indignant rejection of a gay man's offer of a "blow job" in a bar when I was in the navy; another was my enjoyment of gay performers in San Francisco, California and Provincetown, Massachusetts. All of this, and friendships with gay men and women, was generally positive and, I believe, unremarkable, but in my introspection I could sense problems at the edge—an anxious need to preserve a fantasy of a solid absolute barrier with me on one side and Rob on the other. No soft assembly of gender identity (Harris, 1998) for me.

So, along with my generally open-minded liking for and acceptance of Rob and my liberal political orientation was another me inhabited by more of the dominant culture's revulsion for "sissies" and "queers" than I prefer to recognize in myself. My early analytic training reinforced prior prejudices: Homosexuals are neurotic, and paranoids are latent homosexuals. In reviewing the dream image of fist fucker, I felt revulsion at the portrayal itself and more revulsion at the amount of prejudice that had taken root in me. Finally, although I had to dig for it, I found Rob's father in me: I am glad my son is not gay, but if he were, I hope and believe we could each meet the challenge of the Eew factor. In our ending sessions, as a result on my introspection, I believe I was able to contribute more depth to our established intimacy by increased directness and frankness.

Jacob, a college student, began his analysis with great contempt for both analysis and me. He had had a frightening psychotic episode that his hospital therapist believed was drug induced. In the period of his heavy drug use, he had date raped a fellow student who did not report him. He expressed little remorse as he spoke about this episode. However, his psychotic episode deeply frightened him, and despite his overt defiance, he worked within the frame of analysis conscientiously and seriously. His arrogant expressions of hatred toward me at times approached a comic determination to obliterate any possible affectionate feelings from or to me lest he not live up to his father's macho expectations. As Stoller described the extreme macho perspective, "The boy learns that if he is to be considered masculine in our culture, he is expected to be a bad, cocky little sadist" (1975, p. 100). At times, Jacob's attacks had a sadistic quality reminiscent of the tormenting of his younger brother that their parents had done nothing to stop.

The principle challenge to my revulsion came not from his attacks on me but from his abusive demands on his girlfriend for sex. My revulsion took the form of my authoritarian insistence that he look at what he was doing. Something in his desperation awakened me to his suffering. I was able to back off from my heavy-handed demand and take my own advice "to look at what he was doing" empathically. His desperation was not that he saw himself out of control in his demands and forcing behavior, but that he was terrified that I would insist he stop his demands on his girlfriend for sex similar to the demands of his hospital therapist and me having insisted he stop the use of drugs. Exploring his terror at prohibition from aggressive, sometime abusive, pressuring for sex, he told me he believed absolutely that he had to have orgasms or he would become pent up, blow, and go crazy. Although his parents had done nothing to inhibit his abuse of his brother, he felt that the sexual excitement stirred in him by his beautiful, seductive mother was rigorously suppressed by his father's frightening and denigrating attitude toward him. The negative reaction from his father was rarely softened by any affirmation of his masculine development. He hated his own growing recognition that he needed a father who could affirm his masculine strivings, intercede with appropriate prohibitions, and help him to reconsider his pathological behaviors originating from his concretized misconceptions.

Ralph, a medical student, began analysis at the insistence of the medical school. He had been placed on probation when his grades fell to borderline level despite his high intelligence. Much of the early analysis centered on Ralph's rebellious, disdainful attitude toward authorities. His physician father had been demanding, depreciating, and generally unavailable, leaving Ralph to turn toward his mother for support. Ralph was generally shy with women, but with our increased analytic understanding of his problem with authorities, he began tentatively to date. Despite the compulsory nature of his entering treatment, Ralph and I got along well, and I believe he sensed in me a parental (paternal, maternal, or both) hope for him to "spread his wings" not only in school, but also in sensual and sexual areas.

The minicrisis in my response to him involved amazement-revulsion at the form taken in his breakthrough from sexual inhibition. Ralph reported that he had persuaded Dorothy, a girl he had been dating for several months, to do a striptease to stimulate him sexually. Ralph, lying in bed, watched her erotic evocation, and as he reported to me, he did it, he succeeded, and he had had no reaction at all—absolutely no erection. Ralph was triumphant, and I was flabbergasted. My amazement, unlike the direct shaming of dyssmell-revulsion, had the same inhibiting effect. As Tomkins (1987) formulated, when a joyous arousal (Ralph's feeling of triumph) is attenuated, the inhibition (my unspoken "What!") activates shame. Consequently, before we could return to a spirit of inquiry, we each had to recover. Ralph had to recover from his disappointment at my negative mirroring of what he considered a breakthrough from sexual avoidance; I had to recover from what I regarded as a "bizarre" blocking of arousal.

Once we restored our usual working alliance, Ralph could recognize the unusual nature of his triumph and explore with me the meaning of his enactment with Dorothy. When Ralph was 4 or 5 years old, at the height of oedipal longings, his father went away for military service for an extended period. Ralph's mother permitted/invited/seduced him to share her bed. If she sensed or felt him to be aroused, then she would use some excuse to send him away. This prohibition was an implied understanding between them. Explicitly, he remembered that his mother wanted him to be a "quiet" little bed partner. With Dorothy, Ralph enacted his mother's requirement for admission as a desired woman's bed partner. Subsequent to this enactment and our exploration of it, Ralph broke through this prohibition and adopted sexual expressions more derivative of his authentic body desires.

I began describing the experience of sensuality as body sensation-pleasure cocreated and shared between a minutes-old baby, her mother, and her grandfather. A neonate is prepared for experiences of shared sensual pleasure by intrauterine mouth and finger sucking, occasional genital arousal, and skin-to-fluid contact. I differentiated the approving mirroring responses of caregivers that greet the expressions of body sensation pleasure of babies, toddlers, and older children from those caregiver responses of disapproval that shame the child into inhibiting the expression of the desire for bodily pleasure. I characterized as *sexuality* the body sensation desires that have been inhibited-prohibited by shame. *Sensuality* in this distinction involves the search for an expression of body sensation pleasure and later non-body-centered derivatives that are sanctioned and encouraged by parents and authorities and what a specific culture regards as acceptable. In the language of psychoanalytic theories, sensuality would lie in Hartmann's (1939/1958) conflict-free sphere and self-psychology's activities that promote a cohesive sense of self. In contrast, sexuality emerges from conflicting tensions—that between the child's desire for body sensation pleasure and a parent's disapproving inhibition. Rather than the direct explicit activation of pleasure, sexuality requires an individual to regulate his or her desire for body sensation and derivative pleasures between their overt expression, covert expression, or prohibition and suppression. Sexual expression, covert or overt, requires breaking through a barrier triggered by shame, embarrassment, humiliation, shyness, and guilt. Although always intersubjective in origin, the prohibiter-shamer may be experienced as located within or external to the self. Consequently, breaking through may be experienced as against the self or an external agency but must involve assertion or aggression. Thus, sexual expression cannot be entirely "loving" or altruistic. Whatever form an individual's sexual expression takes as it breaks through inhibitions, the lustful desire may or may not follow socially sanctioned patterns and be able to be shared with another individual whose expression also follows a sanctioned path. Sexuality shared in any of the socially sanctioned forms is not in itself of clinical significance except as a possible goal in the analysis of individuals unable to achieve sexual satisfaction and orgasmic release. When pathological prohibition, trauma, and abuse require a breakthrough in which sexuality takes a form (often called perverse) that is hurtful to others and the sense of self, restructuring the form of expression and understanding the factors leading to its choice are often central to a successful analysis. I described five examples of the forms of expression of sexuality by analytic patients that could or did evoke my revulsion (Eew! factor) and required a restoration of the spirit of inquiry to carry the analyses forward.

SENSUALITY IN ADULT ANALYSES

How does sensuality emerge in adult analyses? Commonly, patients talk about their sensuality as a component of affectionate attachments, especially in the form of tender feelings and affectionate physical contact. For adults, sensuality can arise directly from body sensations or more indirectly as an affectionate relational goal that activates the body pleasure aspect through fantasy. Often, patients will mention in passing their enjoyment from bodily experience such as massages, back rubs, sensual handholding, application of oil to the skin, warm baths, or lying in the sun or from more general sensory experiences such as beauty in art and nature. Generally, references to sensuality are shared with analysts as part of a positive attachment or an indicator of progress.

I describe some appearances of sensuality in the five examples of problematic breakthroughs of expressions of sexuality I presented.

Sister Mary's early and continuous battles with her mother fueled her outpourings of hatred and a seeming total absence of body sensation pleasure untainted by antagonism. The governing family myth is that her mother regarded her at birth as big and fat like her father's family, not small, delicate, and refined like the mother and her family. With Sister Mary's weight and size a total liability and source of shame, she could derive no pleasure from the sight of her body or from eating, which was always done by stealth. With the exception of her large-bosomed paternal grandmother and a few nuns, everyone was regarded as an inhibitor or shamer. Based on her experience with her mother, Sister Mary experienced my voice as sandpaper against her skin, my silence as shaming and ostracizing, and my rules, like her father's, as depriving. Alcohol provided what little soothing she could gain. Everything about my office was ugly and tasteless—nothing soft and friendly, like snuggling into her grandmother's bosom had been. She railed against my couch and the art in my office. At the conclusion of her analysis, she had a friend make a cartoon book depicting artwork in my office. The captions were as follows: "I can't be your friend, Joe. I hate Modern Art." "Soon Mary was lonely. She read some books about Modern Art." "She began to understand a little about color and shape." "Mary told Joe what she had learned about his art." "Joe was relieved." "Mary was happy Joe had taught Mary something new." "Mary and Joe became friends again." "The end."

Throughout the lengthy treatment of Mary Jane, I found little evidence of organized experiences of sensuality. Her early life was characterized by neglect and bizarre care from her mother and fear and overstimulation by her raging or seductive father. Her problems with regulation across the spectrum of motivational systems have her functioning between sexual overexcitement, rage episodes, dysfunctional relationships, and generalized daily disorganization. The high points of her existence came from occasional displays of her intellectual brilliance. My reconstruction of her early life was that she was raised by a mother and father with borderline disorders. The episode of sexual abuse as a young teen largely concretized sexuality as an expression of both her desperate pursuit of a secure attachment and the pain-pleasure she experienced from body and emotional contact. In this psychological climate, sensuality as a rich component of her sense of self had little or no way to prosper.

Rob described many experiences of enjoyment of sensual contact with both male and female friends and in aesthetic enjoyment. The general ease of his relationships with others and with me established the contrast to his dream portrayal of me as fist fucker. The view we formed of his childhood was one of a relatively comfortable acceptance of him by both his mother and his father until his revelation of his sexual preference shocked both and drove a painful wedge between him and his father.

In contrast to Rob, who retained and reported many expressions of body sensation and more generalized sensual pleasure, Jacob placed a hard edge of anger–desperate tension on all contacts. He pictured his mother as a beautiful, brilliant, idealized, untouchable woman unresponsive to his "petty" concerns. With unremitting determination, he kept me at arm's length, finding an endless list of reasons to be angry and critical. If nothing else served, then he often accused me of cheating him by arriving half a minute late. Tenderness with anyone was dangerously unmacho, and he persistently was terrified of tenderness, affection, and appreciation of me. Two months before the end of his 7-year successful analysis, I suggested that he could leave hating me, and he would retain his many gains, or he could try out having other feelings. His first reaction was "Nah," but on second thought he said he would see. This opened the door for him to reveal not only more ordinary positive feelings toward me, but also areas of sensual openness with both male and female friends. He volunteered that, as he was leaving this area to work professionally in the west, he wanted to keep "in touch" with me.

Unlike Jacob, who responded to me and the analysis as one more barrier and bad situation with which he was stuck, Ralph saw me as a rescuer who would help him to be reinstated in medical school. Rather than the authorities with whom he was at war, I was allowed to affirm his abilities and to hear of his interest in closeness with friends, travel, and art. I regarded him as drawing on experiences that occurred before his father left and the seductive bed sharing with his mother began. In this preoedipal period, I believe Ralph's parents had supported his sensual pursuits and provided him with a basic sense of acceptance of body pleasure seeking before the dysregulating effect of the later overstimulation and the tug-of-war with his father that ensued after the father's return from service.

Before ending this chapter, I return to my initial question: If sexuality is not the product of a sexual drive, what is it? and offer a preliminary answer that is further developed throughout the book. Sexuality refers to a particular grouping or assembly of pleasure/excitement-oriented behavioral patterns, feelings, fantasies, and conscious and unconscious beliefs about self and self with others. Sexuality develops in response to a wide-ranging group of influences. Basic substrates to sexuality are (a) evolutionary genetic programs designed to ensure reproduction, (b) differentiated male and female body parts and gender-determined generalized propensities, and (c) biologically based inclinations to seek bodily sensations of a pleasurable nature. Based on responses to the basic substrates and the prebirth organization of conscious and unconscious expectations for their child in the mind of each parent, boy and girl infants and parents coconstruct a manner togetherness that enhances the possibility for child and parent to share and enjoy sensual pleasure. As the expressions of sensual pleasure develop and change with the age of the child, parental responses, guided by conscious and unconscious value systems, differentiate acceptable forms of body sensation pleasures from unacceptable forms that elicit reactions of shame and disgust. This is the influence of culture mediated through the individual parents. In comparison to sensuality, sexuality in its initial form is categorized as a shameful prohibited form of expression. A further influence derives from the specific responses to the sex of the child, leading to a primary sense of maleness and femaleness. The relational patterns followed by both genders in pursuit of sensual enjoyment and sexual excitement are heavily influenced by the relational patterns and strategies involved in the child's and parents' attempts to ensure a secure attachment. The gendered self (chapter 3) is coconstructed in a soft assembly that, building on the primary sense of maleness and femaleness, includes different propensities of son or daughter and father and mother communicated explicitly and implicitly. In addition, sensuality and sexuality are influenced by the interplay in childhood between the erotic imaginations of son or daughter and father and mother and in adult life between the erotic imaginations of romantic and sexual partners (chapter 7).

SUMMARY

In this chapter, I place sensuality and sexuality in a self-psychological and relational context. As I have before (Lichtenberg, 1989), I advocate recognition of the distinction between sensuality and sexuality, both developmentally and clinically. I propose that

1. Sensuality is observable from birth on as a wide variety of body sensation pleasures that become a consistent pattern involved in attachment when shared and mirrored by caregivers.
2. Inevitably, some activities of children seeking body sensation pleasure are inhibited by caregivers and are based on value systems of acceptable behaviors guided by caregivers' own lived experiences and cultural does and don'ts.
3. The inhibition of the pleasure seeking activates shame in the child that broadens into a variety of activities that evoke shame or shame-related affects of embarrassment, humiliation, shyness, and guilt.
4. Those body pleasure-seeking activities that elicit shame I refer to as *sexual*.
5. Sexual goals are invariably conflictual (tension laden) in that they represent a struggle between body pleasure seeking-arousal and the inhibiting force of shame and shame-related affects; *sensuality* refers to those body pleasure and aesthetic pursuits that are socially and culturally approved and accepted.
6. When caregivers are sensitive in their inhibition of body pleasure seeking and when the family and culture provide age-appropriate means of sexual expression, the transgressive breakthrough from early defining inhibition of sexual expression takes forms that are not disruptive to the self or to relations with others.
7. When the inhibitions are severe, terrifying, or destructive to self-worth, especially when sexual abuse occurs at any age, the breakthrough of sexual expression may take idiosyncratic forms often called *perversions*, and sensual expression may also be compromised.
8. Some forms of sexual expression evoke revulsion in analysts, an Eew! factor that challenges the analytic work of the dyad.
9. Sensuality is often underappreciated in analysis as an indicator of the patient's conflict-free resources for self-cohesion and relational success.

CHAPTER 2

The Oedipus Complex in the 21st Century

INTRODUCTION

After 100 years of psychoanalytic theorizing about the Oedipus complex, is reconsideration either necessary or valuable? What new perspectives or developmental processes warrant a revised conception? I cite seven changed perspectives that I discuss in detail:

1. The distinction between sensuality and sexuality and the role of culture presented in chapter 1.
2. The complex interplay among interactive, intersubjective, and self-regulation.
3. The continuity since birth (and before) of triadic relationships.
4. The pull exerted on oedipal sexuality by attachment motivations and strategies.
5. The subversive, pernicious, and transgressive influence potential in sexual motives and desires.
6. The role of power, possessiveness, and envy.
7. The maturational influence of a time line of past, present, and future; of an autobiographical organization; and of reflective capacity.

In this chapter, I challenge the view that the oedipal phase is driven by repressed universal unconscious fantasies of sexual possession of the parent of the opposite gender, murder of the rival parent, fear of retaliative castration, or penis envy. I regard the romantic love of the 4- to 6-year-old child as an emergent experience of body sensation and emotional relational desires that takes its form from existent and developing patterns of intrafamily relatedness. The child's patterns of relatedness form as expressions of his or her nonsexual motivations and sensual and sexual desires in the context of continuous influence (regulation) by parental responses both to the child and to each other. At any moment, past patterns of relatedness and present desires congeal into affectively charged lived experiences comprised of patterns of behavior, conscious thoughts and emotions, and elaborations into conscious and unconscious beliefs and fantasies. I describe explicit patterns of intrafamily relationships and the child's implicit modes of relational knowing that develop in sensual and sexual intimate exchanges. Although fantasies importantly elaborate the relatedness patterns of lived experience, neither intrafamily relatedness patterns nor fantasies alone determine the path taken during the oedipal phase. Both explicit and implicit relational patterns and conscious and unconscious fantasies contribute to forming expectations that propel the child into each next moment of lived experience. That said, as I discuss, fantasy elaborations of sexual desires inevitably play out as more or less problematic subversive and transgressive conflicts.

Observational Vignettes

Looking adoringly at his mother all dressed up to go out as she put him to bed, Brian, age 5, said, "Mommy when I grow up I am going to marry you." "No," responded his mother, "When you grow up you will marry someone like me."

What does this ordinary episode of family life indicate? Certainly, that little boys (and girls) 4, 5, and 6 years old experience a juvenile form of romantic love. And, their experience of it may be fully conscious, not some deeply conflicted state. The episode also indicates children of this age have a concept, however vague, of the future—when I grow up. From Brian's mother's side, we can surmise that she probably appreciated the flattering admiration, even adoration, of her and her appearance. Her little man may someday be someone else's lover, but now and for sometime to come, he was hers. She was constrained by her recognition of the need to be accepting and not seductive and so answered him in her culture's "politically correct" response of "someone like me." To Brian, the someone in the future would indeed be the voice of a reality he could appreciate, but that voice would pale in comparison with the fantasy that might accompany his drifting off to sleep, probably fondling his penis. For his mother, the triggering of her fantasy about being adored probably became quickly replaced by the reality of completing her readiness for the evening out with her husband.

Liz, age 6, was engaged in watching a favorite DVD when her father in another room asked her mother to go for an evening walk to see the sunset. Mrs. S., who was in a grumpy mood triggered by a disappointment during the day, declined. Liz called out, "Daddy I'll go with you!" A bit startled but obviously quite pleased, Mr. S. said "Great Liz, get your jacket." As she went past her mother to get her jacket, Liz's face turned from a pleased smile to a look of concern. Turning to her mother, she said "Aw, come on Mom, we'll have fun together," an invitation that, when seconded by Mr. S., shook Mrs. S. out of her indulgence in self-pity and on to the walk.

Without a background context, this vignette is subject to many possible interpretations. Within the moment, Mrs. S. is clearly out of sorts, and her mood places stress on the family's ability to collaborate playfully. Liz, while fully occupied consciously with her DVD, is preconsciously vigilant to the interplay between her parents. Recognizing an opportunity to do something with her father, she eagerly jumped at the chance. Her eagerness clearly indicates the probability of fulfillment of an oedipal desire to be alone with her father and triumph over her rival mother. But, how strong, how central a motivation is the desire to be an oedipal "victor" for this particular little girl? For example, if her mother had agreed to her husband's original invitation to go, would Liz insist on being with her father, unconsciously positioning herself to be close to him, to hold his hand, to vie with mother for his attention and affirmation, knowing what her father wanted to hear, as she praised the sunset? Or, would she have preferred to let her parents have their outing together as she watched her DVD with little or no sense of an opportunity lost?

Was Mr. S. saying, Great I like having company, and I'm glad to have you say yes when your mother says no? Or, was Mr. S. saying, Aha, my little lover is once again coming through for me—we'll have a great time together, better than if that sourpuss came along? Was Mrs. S. saying, Good, let Liz take him off my hands; I don't want to deal with his insensitivity to my disappointment? Was Mrs. S. adding to the more conscious good-riddance-to-them-both feeling an unconscious identification with Liz as an oedipal victor? Was she vicariously imagining herself with her father, winning out over her own mother, who had for years sunk into a general state of pessimism and low-keyed depression? Or, was Mrs. S. simply having a down moment atypical to her usual balanced emotional state so that she was easily jarred out of her momentary sulk by the good feeling that her company was wanted by both her lively daughter and her husband? Even so, was Mrs. S. unconsciously aware of her rivalry with Liz enough to tilt her into not wanting to surrender her place with her husband to her daughter?

The most intriguing questions cluster around Liz's decision to invite her mother to go with her and her father. A classical theory answer would cite a deep unconscious core of guilt: guilt over violation of the incest taboo and guilt over her defeat (fantasized destruction) of her mother. Classical theory somewhat later would add ambivalence between her rivalrous desire to replace her mother and her dependent need for and genuine affection for her, with, in this case, the positive side of her ambivalence winning out.

I believe that traditional theory has understated the strength of the child's desire for an intact family. The powerful affiliative motivation to preserve the integrity of the family group can be recognized in the yearnings of children of divorce and in the stress felt by each family member at a threat of loss. Consequently, I am suggesting the snapshot of Liz and her parents can be interpreted as indicative of oedipal desires exerting a centrifugal (divisive) force on family cohesion, and desires for an intact intimate affiliative attachment exert a centripetal (integrative) force to hold the family together.

Tommy, age 4½, was in the next room playing when his parents were entertaining another couple. The conversation turned to cars, and Tommy's mother began to complain about her car and her husband's unwillingness to replace it. A few heated words were exchanged when Tommy entered, going directly to his mother. He handed her his piggy bank and, in a proud tone, announced he would take her to buy the car she wanted. The adults had a moment of shocked amused silence. After a moment of reflection, Tommy added "But Mommy, you will have to hold my hand as we cross the street."

We can regard Tommy as a classic representative of an oedipal phase 4½-year-old boy acting on his desire to win his mother's love and defeat his rival father in the process. Like Liz, he was vigilantly monitoring his parent's conversation and saw an opening to put his desire into action. The vignette demonstrates the complexity of the child's thinking during this stage. His piggy bank solution for payment for a car demonstrated the immaturity of his knowledge of the world, a lack of which he was oblivious. However, his competitive strategy in itself is sophisticated, but the poignant moment of "hold my hand" comes with his recognition of his lack of ability to perform as an adult. His modeling himself on his father as the man who buys things for his mother (unconscious identification) could carry him so far and then the disparity took hold. This recognition by a child of the reality of his or her limitations, both in general and in sexual performance, is a factor as significant as or more significant than guilt about incest or parenticide in quelling the intensity of oedipal period desires.

The formulations about Tommy that I have just offered are appropriate for a context in which Tommy's parents are having a basically good-natured argument about the car purchase. His mother would be delighted with her little boy lover, and his father would have a mix of surprise, approval, and maybe annoyance.

But, if the context were that the parents squabbled frequently and their alliance was shaky, then Tommy's mother may be actively wooing him to be her precious protector lover, who would share her resentment at her husband, who she regarded as a contemptible cheapskate. Tommy would feel torn between his and his mother's desire for intimacy and his desire for strength-giving masculine identification with his father. Either he tilts toward the needed father, betrays his mother, and becomes an oedipal "loser" or he betrays his own needs for self-strengthening paternal intimacy and then becomes an oedipal loser. I use the term *oedipal loser* here as an abstraction, not a conscious experience. Oedipal loser means (as with so-called boy or girl oedipal winners who "beat out" their rivals) a child whose lived experiences place the child at risk in later life for serious problems in achieving attachment and sensual–sexual intimacy. For a grown-up Tommy, the oedipal loser, I could imagine him as wary of closeness to a woman, fearing entrapment. He might be someone who could "sensitively" pull a woman into an attachment/sexual intimacy only then to abandon her to cover his doubts about sustaining the relationship. I could imagine him drawn to powerful men, with whom he played out various forms of domination–submission enactments while always vulnerable to doubting his manliness.

For Tommy, the little boy whose parents really get along and were having a good-natured spat about the car and who delighted in the charm of his precocious offer of rescue and who was neither oedipal winner nor loser, I could imagine him successfully negotiating later relationships with both a woman he desired and men with whom he competed or developed friendships. I recognize that such imagined outcomes are highly conjectural because many variables in adolescence and adulthood can affect negatively or positively the path launched by the oedipal period proclivities.

Tessa, age 5, squealed "No" when her father, older brother, and sister invited her to go to the beach with them. Tessa immediately went over to her mother, looking downcast as her brother and sister teased her about being mommy's little baby girl. Tessa and her mother, both overweight, stood immobilized, in contrast to the energetic activity of the other three athletic family members. Two years before Tessa's birth, her mother, Mrs. B., had a miscarriage, and her own mother had died. Her affect during her pregnancy with Tessa was a mix of anxiety and depression. In her state of withdrawal, Mrs. B. and her husband lived parallel lives, as considerate of one another as they could be but without any of the romantic love and sexual ardor that had been present when the older two children were born. After Tessa's normal birth, Mrs. B., in momentary relief, turned to the baby and to food as her principal source of affection and security. Upset if Tessa cried, Mrs. B. frequently had Tessa in bed with her despite Mr. B.'s objections. At preschool and kindergarten, after overcoming the difficulties of separation with the help of her mother, who really wanted Tessa to develop intellectually, Tessa (as bright and essentially as competent as her accomplished siblings) did well. Only on return home did she regularly succumb to the regressive pull of existence as her mother's central focus of preoccupation. I conjecture that Tessa's oedipal phase experience provided her with painfully little opportunity for joyous intersubjective play with her father, a chance to enter the game of triadic heterosexual wins and losses. The vignette reveals nothing of Tessa's bodily experience, her masturbatory patterns, and her sensual or erotic fantasies and how much sexual and sensual pressure from within was propelling her to extricate herself from her preoccupation with her mother and food. The vignette does reveal the relational problem of insecure interdependent attachment and sensual enmeshment with her mother. With no gleam in her mother's eyes toward her father, she had no beacon to lead her into oedipal heterosexuality but regrettably did have strong attachment pulls against it.

NEW PERSPECTIVES

Returning to my original questions (After 100 years of psychoanalytic theorizing about the oedipal complex, is reconsideration either necessary or valuable? What new perspectives or developmental processes warrant a revised conception?) I suggest that, in the snapshot vignettes, I have already indicated a number of perspectives to add to the skeletal structure of the observation that boys and girls 4 to 6 years of age have romantic desires toward a parent, generally the opposite sex parent, and are restrained in the full enactment of their desire by fear of punishment for violation of a culturally enforced incest taboo, guilt over destructive fantasies toward their parent rival, need for an affectionate attachment to the rival parent, and a recognition of the child's physical and functional limitations. I am deliberately not including castration anxiety and penis envy in the core skeletal structure. Some boys may fear that girls had and lost their penis and that it could happen to them, and some girls may believe that possession of a penis would repair any sense of inadequacy they have. Such fantasies and unconscious beliefs have a significant role to play in the formidable list of mysteries that can befuddle a child's comprehension of sexuality. However, in ordinary development, castration anxiety and penis envy do not occupy the pivotal roles for ending the oedipal phase via repression that Freud (1915) assigned to them.

I now discuss each of the seven changed perspectives I cited in the opening section.

The Distinction Between Sensuality and Sexuality and the Role of Culture

In chapter 1, I presented the evidence for a distinction between *sensuality* in the form of socially sanctioned pleasurable body sensations and fantasies and *sexuality* in the form of socially disapproved of pleasurable body sensations and fantasies. A boy or girl coming into the oedipal phase has already acquired an extensive set of explicit and implicit rules about sensual desires openly to be enjoyed with others or while alone, and other rules about sexual desires not openly to be enjoyed with others, maybe allowable when alone and maybe not. A little girl may be allowed to take a shower with her mother and openly enjoy the shared nudity and pleasurable sensations but not be allowed to touch and explore her mother's genitals, no matter how enticing a stimulus so near to the little girl's eye level.

Some rules are variably enforced and potentially confusing to a child. Emily was allowed by her parents to fondle her genital area while lolling on the sofa watching television, but when her grandparents visited, she received a shocked reaction and a strong rebuke. Does a bedrock of absolute prohibition exist? Is it the hypothetical universal incest taboo? Anthropologists believe it to be a universal value but, like many such universal values (thou shall not kill), often is violated. Sroufe, Egeland, and Carlson (2005) observed a group of mothers who "passionately kiss toddlers, rub their buttocks, genitals, or stomachs in a sensual way; plaintively asking for kisses; bribe with kisses; and whisper and call to them in ways that were obviously sensual" (p. 45). These maternal behaviors were directed almost exclusively to boys and occurred when the child was not complying. On testing, these mothers showed lower warmth and higher hostility than other mothers did. The authors noted that the seductive behavior was "strongly related to a history of the mother having been treated sexually by an adult male in childhood" (p. 45). However, the mothers were repeating not only a set of learned behaviors but also a pattern of relating. They did not replicate the identical forms of seduction that were done to them by their fathers. Rather, they engaged in culturally dictated female counterparts. Interestingly, these same mothers did not necessarily behave seductively toward another son, and, with daughters, rather than using seductive behavior, they would behave in a hostile, derogatory, or demeaning manner. The authors concluded that, in their depreciation of their daughters, they were reconstructing the depreciatory pattern of the way they had been treated. Sroufe et al.

used three descriptors for the large number of woman they studied: those having a positive identification with a competent mother; those identified with a chaotic, disorganized, harsh troubled mother; and those whose identity was of existence as a "spousified" daddy's girl when young and later as identified with father. The authors strongly adhered to a family systems approach: "Relational learning involves incorporating an entire family system—how the child was treated by a father figure and by a mother, and how the adults treated each other" (p. 16).

The Interplay Among Interactive, Intersubjective, and Self-Regulation

For a long time, psychoanalysis struggled with resolving the dichotomy between Freud's abandoned theory of strangulated affects and repressed memories of actual traumas (an external influence causing psychopathology) and his later theory of drive distortion (solely internal influence) that was regarded as dogma during my training. The dichotomy between internal and external influence took many forms: intrapsychic versus interpersonal, drive versus relationship, sexual and aggressive instinct versus attachment. This unresolved battle of theories did little to change the classic view that in early development the child went through a series of phases: oral, anal, phallic, and oedipal. Each succeeding phase influenced the formation of psychic structure through a mixture of drive-fulfillment fantasy distortion and increasing but limited capacity for reality testing. Psychosexual stage development moved forward in an average expectable environment. In the average expectable environment, the inevitable unresolved conflicts that would play out in adult life were created by the desires, fears, guilt, and ambivalence of the oedipal complex. In terms of an analogy to research, analysts were saying that one variable, external reality (what parents actually did), could be held as a constant, and the other variable, intrapsychic developmental progression, could be mapped in all its intricacies.

The increasing incontrovertible evidence from every study of pathology—both attachment research and child observation and clinical analysis—points to the frequency of emotional disturbances and dysfunction within families as well as physical and sexual abuse of children. Arguing that the source of conflict and pathology is both internal and external removes the dichotomy but does not explain how each functions to bring about either adaptive or maladaptive development. For that, a systems approach is needed. A system (the oedipal configuration) organizes based on (a) the little girl's desire for her father (her self-system), (b) the father's empathic response to her overtures (his self-system), and (c) the exchanges between them of shared looks, holding hands, and the like (their dyadic system). The system stabilizes based on repetition: The little girl comes to expect a regularity in her father's joy at her rushing to the door as he comes home, her unconscious monitoring of the time or the sound of his car and footstep. The father's positive expectation leads him to regularize their exchange, clear his head of other concerns, and with each exchange adds an accretion of positive feeling to their relationship that serves as a resource for recovering from disappointments. The system exists in dialectic tension: The little girl is angry that her father has told her she is getting too big (old) to sit on his lap to watch a movie (her expectation must be revised). The father has become aware that her movements and bits of fondling have moved for him (and he expects for her) from sensuality comfortable for both to sexuality (penis arousal) inappropriate for both. The disruption in their pattern demands a reorganization of their exchanges to restore their positive affective intersubjectivity. The system undergoes hierarchical reorganization; able to be intuitively reflective about both her and her father's feelings, the little girl reaches for a more mature form of being with daddy. She sits beside him on the sofa. Appreciative of her solution, he relaxes, and the new cocreated ambiance includes shared admiration on both sides.

I can describe patterns of interactive regulation and self-regulation and their interplay more abstractly. Dyadic interactive regulation involves each partner communicating to the other the degree of emotional closeness and distance, intimacy, and attachment each wants with and from the other. The dyadic communicative exchanges involve words, body language, tone, vocal rhythm, and expressions of empathic understanding or misunderstanding. Self-regulation involves the continuous regulation of affect and arousal by heightening attention or diminishing vigilance. Self-regulation employs and revises expectations and works to preserve safety while negotiating desire. Self-regulation functions via articulated anticipation and planning as well as fantasy and bodily means of homeostasis (self-fondling, sighs, yawns, scratching, restlessness, drowsiness, eating).

Self- and interactive regulation are simultaneous, constantly reorganizing, updating, negating, or reinforcing the sense of self and the sense of self with other. An additional clarification is needed. The dyadic interaction is not linear as it might seem from ordinary descriptive language sequencing: The little boy flirts with his mother, she notices and teases that he is her dinner partner with daddy away. He struggles to regulate his slightly hurt feelings about the teasing. A superficial external observer's view would be that this is a linear procession of A leads to B followed by C. Nonlinear sequencing is more like the process of two mating animals. Each animal knows the other's "moves," so that each move includes an anticipation of what the other will do while each simultaneously makes the internal regulations necessary to maximize the opportunity to achieve their shared goal. Another analogy is to two drivers approaching on a two-lane road. Each is regulating personal attention to monitor the sensory information needed to ensure that the other is following an expected pattern, and each has also increased vigilance in case of a sudden breach of expectation. To add yet another dimension to self- and interactive regulation, a child's perception is not confined to monitoring external communications from the parent and simultaneously regulating the self in response to it, either to comply or to oppose. The child also receives messages of varying intensity from the body, signaling hunger, restlessness, sensual–sexual arousal, and so on. Thus, the contemporary concept of a cocreation of lived experience implies the coexistence of multiple influences operating simultaneously but does not address the relative power of influence of any one factor. Finally, ongoing regulation is affected by the distinction between interactive (procedural, what to do) and intersubjective (emotion-centered) communications. A kindergarten traffic safety guide provides valuable information with go or wait signals for the children's interactive regulation. The guide may notice a little boy's timidity and with empathic sensitivity offer him reassurance—an intersubjective regulation. For an oedipal age child, intersubjective regulation, more than interactive, is crucial for the child's regulation of gender identity. How the child's father and mother regard masculinity and femininity, their own and their partners, and what they wish for their child will affect their empathic capacity to enter into and enhance the child's internal regulation of his or her gender identity and acceptance of masculine and feminine aspects.

The Continuity Since Birth (and Before) of Triadic Relationships

Recognition of the significance of the family system for the oedipal phase child is a recent development in psychoanalysis. Kleinian theory, by placing the oedipal complex much earlier than the age of 4 to 6 years, introduced triadic relations much earlier than other schools that distinguish among preoedipal, largely dyadic, relations and oedipal phase triadic relations. Fivaz-Depeursinge and Corboz-Warnevy (1999) studied mother–father–infant groups in a play setting when the baby was 3, 6, 9, and 12 months of age. The experimental design revealed the ability of the parents to work with each other and the baby. The parents were instructed each to play with the baby sequentially, with the other observing or assisting, parents were to engage each other, and then all were to play together. Because the four play modes were to be accomplished in a fixed time limit, the parents had to apportion the times to shift from one play pattern to the next. The experimenters found that the families fell into four groups: those who cooperated well, those who were able to overcome stress successfully, those in which one or the other attempted to collude to include one and exclude another, and those who were chaotic and disorganized. The initial 3-month classifications were reconfirmed throughout the test period. Looked at from the baby's standpoint, one group of parents knew how to act with each other and with the infant to play in both a dyadic and a triadic manner. Another group could overcome the stress created by one member (e.g., an overstimulating mother or an emotionally flat father or a fussy baby) and coconstruct a positive play experience. In a third group, one parent or the other attempted to seduce the baby (or the other parent) into a dyadic collusion at the expense of the left-out person, thereby eliminating the possibility of the family's ability to enjoy each other fully as a unit. The fourth group operated in a manner that did not permit a reliable pattern to occur in which any one member's desire for play could be met and a positive affective state involving all members be created and sustained. This research confirms that triadic relations are present at birth but raises questions about the power of the factors involved: the baby's temperament; the parents' prior relationship with each other; the prior, especially early, lived experience of each parent. To answer some of these questions the experimenters tested families during a first-time pregnancy. The prospective parents were asked to play with a genderless doll as if it were their baby-to-be. Remarkably, the classifications of the prebirth "family" groupings proved predictive of the categories in the postbirth testing.

D. Diamond and Yeomans (2007) referred to a study by Klitzing, Simons, and Burgin (1999) that tested first-time parents' prebirth capacity to envision postnatal triadic familial relationships. A parent's ability to envision a relationship in which neither the self nor the partner was excluded from the relationship with the infant predicted the success of triadic play interactions with the child at 4 months of age. Diamond and Yeomans added that multiple investigations suggest that the actual triangular relationships and the parent's own oedipal/triangular representations influence the child's development from birth. The studies also speak to the trend to deemphasize oedipal wishes and fantasies as independently originating intrapsychic phenomena and to focus on how parental sexuality and the parental couple are registered internally by the child.

As a consequence of the organizing power of the triadic family system, the dyadic system examples I presented to illustrate how systems organize, stabilize, and undergo dialectic tension and hierarchical reorganization would benefit from triadic reconsideration. The little girl's dyadic system with her father holding hands and sharing looks would actually be a triadic system encouraged or discouraged by her mother. Her mother could cooperate with her daughter and husband's playful flirtation, enter into it, and protect her self-interest as the other two cooperate with her. In the stabilizing of the dyadic relationship at the door as the father comes home from work, the mother could cooperate by giving her eager daughter and her husband their moment with each other. This might require a momentary suppression of her self-interest to get there first to tell her husband her news of the day. In the ending of the eroticized lap sitting, the mother might cooperate by sharing in her judgment of the appropriateness, she might be stressed by her resentment of their closeness, or she might be unconsciously reliving her own oedipal erotic fantasies via her daughter, having unconsciously colluded to facilitate the activity. My point is that to understand preoedipal or oedipal age events, we must recognize the existence of both a dyadic and a triadic regulatory perspective because both coexist in the family system even before birth.

The Pull Exerted on Oedipal Sexuality by Attachment Motivations and Strategies

Although dyadic and triadic relationships coexist even before birth, analytic theory has privileged dyadic relations in the preoedipal period and triadic relations in the oedipal phase. I consider now how the dyadic strategies worked out in attachments in infancy have an impact on later triadic relations. Bowlby's (1958) adherence to an evolutionary perspective gave complete primacy to the coming together of helpless infant and caregiving mother to provide the child with a secure base at times of danger and loss. Whatever other relational interactions infants have, the central force of their experiential world is on the primary caregiver whose protective presence and ministrations are required for their survival. A central motivation for infants is to form patterns of relating that ensure the continuity of their attachment. By 1 year of age, patterns of relating to ensure safety are organized in categories of secure and insecure attachments. Because these patterns or strategies are basic implicit and explicit ways of relating, they inevitably influence the child's mode of interacting when motivations other than attachment are dominant. The strength of the influence will vary; for example, a child's intense desire to explore may override his preoccupation with his mother and at preschool leave him able to play with toys and peers without repeating negative patterns of relating with his teacher. Or, unhappily, his entire focus may be on the teacher.

How might the patterns of secure and insecure attachment influence the manner in which sensual–sexual system motivations become manifest in the oedipal phase? This question cannot be answered without expanding attachment theory beyond the limited goal of seeking proximity with a caregiver at times of danger and loss. Infants and mothers seek proximity with each other (a) for security (to go from a negative affect of fear to a positive affect of safety); (b) to have a multitude of physiological needs met, to indulge in playful interactions of all sorts, to experience mirroring affirmation, a sense of sharing and commonality, and the flow of mutual admiration and idealization (i.e., to activate and regulate many experiences of positive affect, including sensuality); and (c) to gain and communicate information, especially about who each is to the other and how to optimize their moment-to-moment experience and overcome obstacles to successful relating through empathy. Accordingly, secure attachment implies that the child (a) has learned to appeal to the mother when frightened by danger or absence and anticipate and receive a comforting acceptance and sensual hold and hug and (b) to share a multitude of pleasurable experiences, what Holmes (2007) calls hedonic intersubjectivity and Lieberman, St. John, and Silverman (2007) refers to as the positive qualities of dependence. Holmes stated that what makes a secure base secure is its physicality, the warmth, holding, feeling, reassuring heartbeat, soothing words, and gentle touch desired by both child and parent. Carrying forward into oedipal phase and later affectionate interactions, kissing, cuddling, tickling, holding, mutual gazing, stroking, and playfulness all contribute a sensual linkage between dyadic and triadic intersubjectivity. For Lieberman et al., recognition of affectively positive dependent experiences alerts us to the passion inherent in an emotional hierarchy that places a unique and irreplaceable maternal figure at the center of the child's love life. The key concepts expressed here are the link between the child's passionate love of mother inherent in secure attachment and the child's later (oedipal, adolescent, and adult) romanticized, sensual, and sexual triangular love affairs.

But, what consequences for oedipal phase relations derive from failures in maternal empathy and patterns of insecure attachment? What follows if the principal figure in the child's life responds to signals of need inconsistently, sometimes receptively and sometimes angrily rejecting? Impelled by an inchoate sense of romantic affection and encouraged by moments of receptivity, the oedipal age child will continue to approach the parent of desire unsure both of the parent's response and of his or her own ability to elicit the desired affection. Rather than the relatively easy and direct approach of the securely attached child, the ambivalently attached child will struggle with preoccupations of whether his mother (or her father) returns his (or her) love and desire. What trust can he (or she) place in his father's (or mother's) affectionate support rather than rivalrous humiliation? Is he (or she) good enough, big enough, attractive enough to be loved in return for his (or her) romantic affection? Frequently, patterns of taking care of a parent (role reversal) or acting babyish conflate attachment goals and sexual goals—with either used in pursuit of the other.

If the principal figure in an infant's life responds to signals of need with cold detachment, contempt, or dismissive anger, then the child will develop a strategy of suppressing direct appeal and often suppressing indications of protest as well. With this attachment background, when pressed by desire, the oedipal age child will often remain avoidant of direct approaches while withdrawing into autoerotic states of masturbation and fantasy. The child's inner world tends to be colored by domination–submission fantasies, giving both desire and rivalry a sadomasochistic flavor, often acted out in peer relations.

If the principal figure in an infant's life responds to signals of need by superimposing personal states of affective disturbance (anger, fear, depression, ineptitude, sexual neediness), then the infant may be unable to form a coherent strategy so that lapses of disorientation, disorganization, and dissociation occur at moments of dysregulated arousal. The oedipal age child may approach the parent of desire either avoidantly or ambivalently or alternatively with moments of breakthrough of affective dysregulation. The child may be prone to overreact to disappointment and be overtly antagonistic to one or both parents. If sexual abuse has been a part of the attachment trauma, then oedipal age girls may become little vamps, overtly and aggressively seductive, and both boys and girls may be controlling and demanding, treating one or both parents as servants to gratify any wish or desire.

Most analytic theoreticians regard the attachment and the sensual–sexual systems as having different evolutionary roots—one to ensure safety, the other to ensure reproduction—and as having different experiential patterns of behavior and emotions. I have looked at how the dyadic patterns of attachment strategies that were formed in infancy affect the oedipal age child's sensual and sexual triadic experiences. Crossover influences between the two systems exist from birth. Affection is affection whether expressed as a baby's love for the mother who makes her feel safe and her tummy feel good, expressed as a toddler's admiration for his daddy who can lift him up high in the air excitedly, or expressed as a 5-year-old's loving romantic feeling when sitting next to her father on the sofa. The depth of love, the fullness of a child's sense of openness to passion in any form, is affected by whether attachment is experienced as secure or insecure. Alternatively, the affection generated by sexual longings and a good experience during the oedipal period can provide an insecurely attached child another opportunity to gain attachment closeness. Many children, adolescents, and adults who have had insecure attachments utilize sensual and sexual linkages to achieve attachment goals.

Another crossover between the two systems lies in the duality of experience each child has with each parent as a gendered figure. A mother not only is a central attachment figure but also is a source of information about femininity, taken in implicitly by identification (conscious and unconscious modeling) and explicitly as schemas of little girl-with-feminine-mother to be compared with schemas of little girl-with-masculine-father. A father not only is another figure with whom the child forms an attachment pattern independently but also is a source of information about masculinity taken in implicitly by identification and explicitly as schemas of little boy-with-masculine-father to be compared with schemas of little boy-with-feminine-mother. Concurrent with her principal attachment pattern with her mother and her additional attachment pattern with her father, a little girl is acquiring implicit knowledge of being feminine like mother and ordinarily to a lesser degree being masculine like father. Concurrent with his primary attachment pattern with his mother and his additional attachment pattern with his father, a little boy is acquiring implicit knowledge of being masculine like father and ordinarily to a lesser degree being feminine like mother. "Terms like 'masculinity' and 'femininity' are very context sensitive, taking on a distinct coloration and particular network of meaning within particular life-worlds.... Feminine qualities or experience will likely be distinct and different in a man or in a woman" (Harris, 2000, p. 230). Harris noted that Corbett (1993) argued that femininity in gay men is not identical to femininity in a woman.

The Subversive, Pernicious, and Transgressive Influence Potential in Sexual Motives and Desires

In this section, I describe the conflictual twist to romantic love that derives from the culturally driven dichotomy between socially accepted sensuality and the inherent potential in sexual expression of shame and guilt. Stated differently, a subversive, pernicious, transgressive influence is potential in the pressure from body sensation pleasure and erotic fantasy and the concurrent restraint or prohibition. In Freudian terms, this would be a conflict of id versus superego, strictly an intrapsychic event. My belief is that the entire experience, rather than a strictly internal process, is cocreated dyadically and triadically. Two hooks define the child's dilemma. One hook is that life is full of inciter-attractors. An itch is to scratch. A hurt is to cry about. A nipple, a finger, a toe is to suck.

A full bladder or a full rectum is to empty. A stuffed nose is to pick at. A mouth is to kiss. A genital is to fondle and rub against. A pigtail is to pull. A little brother standing quietly is for a big brother to agitate. A stone, a pea, or a ball is to throw. A breast or a bottom is to fondle. A naked body is to peer at. A skirt is to look under. Genitals are to display with pride. A wall is to draw on. Bedroom sounds are to listen to and fantasize about.

The other hook is the interplay the action taken or anticipated evokes/provokes in a parent (the dyadic system) and in the broader family/culture (a triadic or multiple-individual system). Parents acting as authorities respond differently to disapproved-of actions perceived to be driven by body excitement from the way they do to other disapproved-of actions perceived to be assertive, destructive, or defiant. A mother who wants to prohibit her 5-year-old son from pulling a visiting girl's pigtail will look him straight in the eye, point her finger at him, and unambivalently tell him in no uncertain terms to stop. The look from his father may fully back up mother or contain a wink and a nod that boys will be boys. A mother who enters her daughter's bedroom as the 5-year-old little girl jerks her hand from under the covers may look away in shameful embarrassment, mumble something like "Don't," and be made uncomfortable and uncertain about her daughter's masturbation. The message to the little girl is that she is doing something she should not be doing, that it makes her mother (and her) uncomfortably anxious to have to deal with it, and that the something wrong is clearly different from the something wrong with breaking a dish or defacing a book. The father in a similar circumstance with the 5-year-old girl is apt to be even more awkward in his embarrassed turning away. Of course, parents might respond to a male or female oedipal child in a vast variety of ways, including delivering a harangue about sin and damnation and threats of castration or becoming insane. I argue that in all the responses, from the embarrassed turning away to the violent threat, the parent consciously or unconsciously means to convey that these doings with bodily excitement are different from other "naughty" doings. They constitute a particular regulatory bugaboo called *sex*.

The prohibited bodily excitement pursuits are subversive of the child's belief in the validity of the dictates of authority. An oedipal age child can accept that an authority is correct that a plate should be held more carefully so as not to drop it, or that the boy really hurts the little girl whose pigtail he pulls. The child's empathic understanding can tilt with education to the side of the authority as mentor. Going with the authority against the full "truth" of the body message "it feels so good" is made more difficult by two factors: (a) the persistent strength of the body message, particularly centering on genital sensation intensified by the power of curiosity about the mysteries of procreativity in the oedipal period (and again in puberty); and (b) the inevitable conscious or unconscious ambivalence of the parent, who for all his or her life has received similar body pleasure messages and been curious.

A solution used by authority is to find a half measure of sexual expression that works for the age of the child and the current culture, such as you can "touch yourself in the privacy of your room but not in public, and here is a book about where babies come from." Half measures leave problems. The child masturbating in the privacy of his or her room still feels that he or she is doing something "wrong," that he or she is transgressive, and generally the child retains the desire to transgress further (e.g., in bathroom play with another child) because transgressing itself adds to excitement. The child reading the sanitized version of procreation remains curious about how to connect his or her body experience and knowledge with an inevitably impenetrable set of puzzles about intercourse, sperm, ovaries, uteruses, menstrual cycles, and ejaculation. The desire to transgress the proscribed boundaries to satisfy curiosity persists with ample opportunity for peeking, looking, staring, and showing as provided by television ads, movies, magazines, the Internet, and public bathrooms. My 6-year-old daughter, when taken to the movie *Funny Girl* and on seeing a partially explicit scene of the seduction of Fanny Brice in a private dining room, shouted out, "How did he get her in that position?" to the consternation of her parents and the amusement of the audience.

Each child in interplay with one or both parents is learning moment to moment what he or she can do and win approval; what he or she can do and get away with; what he or she can get away with unless caught; what he or she knows is absolutely forbidden to do but does not personally accept as forbidden because he or she does not believe it is wrong to do; and what he or she knows is both absolutely forbidden and accepts (at least for the time being) that it is wrong to do.

Nancy's (Lichtenberg, Lachmann, & Fosshage, 1996) mother's response to Nancy's protest that her older brother was rubbing "himself" against her (masturbating first against her leg and then on top of her) was to tell Nancy that none of it would happen if Nancy played with her dolls and stayed away from her brother (the only child available for play). Nancy learned that her brother could do whatever he wanted to her. Nancy, whose attachment to her mother was ambivalent-preoccupied, learned that she risked whatever security she could get from her mother if she demanded protection. Nancy learned that her father would not involve himself with supervising his children and was satisfied with encouraging Nancy's nascent sexuality as long as it was directed at him. Nancy mainly learned that she was guilty no matter what desire she followed. If she wished to stay near mother and watch her put on makeup, then she was told she was too intrusive and dependent. If she followed her father into the bathroom to be with him before he went to work, then he welcomed her until she was too overtly intent on looking at his penis, and then he chased her out. If she followed her mother's instructions and stayed in her room playing with her dolls, then her brother, jealous of the loss of her interest in him, cut off the doll's arms. The inference Nancy drew from her experience was that girls are inherently evil, draw men into doing bad things, and are forbidden to express their desires; men have all the freedom and fun.

Moving beyond the oedipal period of Nancy's experience to her analysis as an adult to make my point about the subversive, pernicious, transgressive aspect of sexuality, Nancy as an adult was a highly principled, ethical person whose general convictions of existence as a good religious person were subverted by the unrelenting (pernicious) nature of her unfulfilled attachment and romantic sexual desires. Following her attachment pattern of preoccupation-ambivalence, she involved herself with a series of flirtations and affairs in which the situation was characterized by ambiguity: who was the instigator and who the follower, who was available and who not, who wanted the other to commit while he or she played the "teaser." For analysis, the valuable side of the continuity of these preoedipal and oedipal problems and the pressure to break through the inhibiting constraints transgressively lies in the opportunity to re-create the experiences outside and inside the analytic dyad so they can be explored and opened to creative change. Although analysis will explore many different relational thrusts, sexual desire, with its persistent clamor to be heard, often provides the lead in reconstructing not only sensual–sexual problems but also problems in attachment.

Although the adult Nancy would and did enter into a clinical exchange based on inquiry and affective transformation, oedipal period children can go but so far with the underlying mysteries. Will a monster in the closet catch them for sexual transgressions? Will an omnipotent being, the parent or God, see their every move and hold them tightly to account? Will she get pregnant if she touches a boy's penis? Does the girl's different genital area mean a penis can be lost? If sexual intercourse means entry, then is the girl's body, the hard-to-see and fully appreciate slit, able to accommodate what must go into it, or will she be hurt, be torn up? How can babies as big as they are come out of the small opening a girl/woman seems to have? Is the vagina really separate, or is it "dirty"—connected to the anus, a cloaca? Will little penises ever get big enough to do what they have to do, and when? Why is it exciting for a boy to be around a little girl, and what should he do or not do? Why is it also exciting for a boy to be around another boy, and what should he do or not do? Why is it exciting for a girl to be around a little boy, and what should she do or not do? Why is it exciting for a girl to be around another little girl, and what should she do or not do? Clearly, no oedipal age child can resolve these puzzles, and I dare say many, if not most, adults struggle with vestiges of them. Thus, sexuality always retains a special feel, a special claim of subversiveness to the good order of "rationality" and transgressiveness to the good rules of "etiquette" and manners. Sexuality and anality have a "dirty talk" language of their own.

Securely attached oedipal age children and their autonomous parents will have an easier time dealing with these conundrums; insecurely attached oedipal age children and their preoccupied or avoidantly attached parents will have a more difficult time. For example, Lieberman, St. John, and Silverman (2007) described two examples of the difficulties oedipal age children have with parents who explicitly exploited the child's dependence on them. Following Harris, Lieberman et al. (2000) noted that the child's body offers densely textured meanings and affects that trigger the parent's conscious and unconscious fantasies. The extreme power imbalance in the parent–child relationship, coupled with the child's emotional need for the parent, expose the child to the parent's psychological vulnerabilities and erotic characterological pathology.

One bulimic mother, convinced that her 4-year-old daughter, Tina, was too chubby and food focused, enrolled Tina in a gymnastics class the child did not enjoy. The mother sat on the mat eating a pastry while instructing Tina to pay attention to the teacher. She complained that Tina whined constantly that she was hungry and masturbated frequently, embarrassing her mother. Lieberman et al. (2007) made a valuable contribution to the multidimensional purposes of masturbation. Via masturbation, they noted that Tina attempted (a) to gather her attention in, engage her body, and physically drown out her mother's distracting presence; (b) to regulate herself affectively, maintain a sense of bodily awareness, and take possession of her own body: and (c) to engage her repelled and riveted mother in emotionally charged exchanges. I would add that Tina was also expressing her transgressive desire for a pleasant bodily sensation at a time of disinterest, boredom, hunger, envy, and resentment.

Lieberman et al. (2007) also described Angela, who at 3 years old was treated for separation anxiety and excessive interest in her father's genitals. Angela's father triggered her intense attachment insecurity by insisting that she be left behind as he and his sometimes-reluctant wife went on trips. He then complained about Angela's neediness and manipulative nature. He established a highly sexual relationship with her, dancing with her, videotaping her, and encouraging her to show "how sexy she was." He allowed her to go into the bathroom to watch him urinate but unpredictably would yell at her to get out. From the age of 5 years, Angela demanded morning reports of the parent's sexual activity the previous night, with father compliant and mother opposed.

Preoedipal and oedipal period dyadic and triadic experiences such as those of Nancy, Tina, and Angela lay bare the subversive, pernicious, and transgressive aspects of sexuality that become accentuated by the exploitative sexual motives and desires of parents and siblings in concert with those of the vulnerable child. The subversive and transgressive influence will play out in dramatic fashion in adolescence, as documented for Angela, and in adulthood, as documented for Nancy.

I end this section with two conjectures that require further clinical research. First, a major loss for exploited and abused children lies in the absence of a healthy domain of sensuality so important for nonerotic friendship, affection, and intimacy, a domain that successful analysis can promote. Second, even when the oedipal phase triadic relationships are fully supportive and the children retain full comfortable access to their sensuality, especially during adolescence and episodically during adulthood, an upsurge of lustful desire will inevitably subvert attention away from nonsexual motives and evoke conflict with some carryover of childhood ethical and moral injunctions. For adolescents and adults, romantic love requires a degree of transgressive exploration and experimentation to cope with the prohibitions that originate from the anxiety-driven parental shaming that separates sensuality from sexuality.

The Role of Power, Possessiveness, and Envy

Power and its distribution plays a part in all epochs of life, and it certainly is a factor in sensuality, for which it is shared, and in sexuality, for which it may be shared or inflicted in patterns of domination–submission intrusion. When questioned about the interest he evoked in attractive women, Henry Kissinger famously answered, "Power is an aphrodisiac." I discuss power during the oedipal phase as it applies to possessiveness or possession and to the manner in which power triggers envy, admiration, and idealization.

Mothers put Q-tips in infants' and toddlers' ears; shove nipples or spoons in their mouths; place thermometers, suppositories, and enema tubes up their anus; hoist them up when they want to remain on the ground to play; put them down when they want to be held; pull their hands off of body parts they are fondling; brush their hair painfully; tickle them until it hurts; and scrub the genital area obsessively. Lieberman et al. (2007) described a father who practiced physiotherapy massage on his naked infant daughter in front of a group. So, a child can easily wonder, "Whose body is it anyway? Do I have control of my orifices? Can I self-regulate my body surfaces to feel sensual pleasure?"

An important component of preoedipal experience is the child's establishing a sense of agency that comes from both an expectation that her desire will be responded to so that satisfaction is achievable and an expectation that her aversiveness will be recognized and negotiated. The child enters the oedipal phase with a greater or lesser degree of confidence in his or her agency in general. When it comes to those bodily desires that are proscribed as "sexual don'ts," the child may wonder to what degree pieces and parts of his or her body and the desires that originate from them have been forfeited to a parent or parents. Possessiveness can go both ways; a mother can be so submissive to her child's wishes that the child concludes that the mother is the child's possession, a slave. This is an early contribution to a sense of entitlement that can destroy future relations. Or, a mother can be so unresponsive and unaccommodating to her child's wishes that the child concludes he or she has no claim on the mother, no sense of the possessive "my" in "my mother."

Oedipal age children are sensitive observers of patterns of possession—not only toys but also especially those involved in triadic romantic love. A 5-year-old boy will look at his father and mother kissing and sort out whether the father owns her (she is only kissing him because he demands it), she owns him (he is only responding to her overtures because she demands it), or if there is mutuality between them and, in a manner of speaking, they own each other. Whichever it is, where does that leave him? If mother only responds to father because he demands it and responds to the child eagerly, then is she his? If mother only responds to father and to him because of demand, then she could be regarded as a possession of either, but is a person without desire and thereby a "devalued" property. For both boy and girl, the permutations are endless and alterable based on life changes. The constant is that in all love relations many preoccupations and fantasies inevitably emerge from the question of who belongs to whom. Adult forms of erotic imagination, especially in the physical union of bodies in intercourse, elaborate fantasies of merger in which bodies are treated as boundaries and selves as territory to cede to another and retake for one's own, especially in the playing out of penetration and receptivity.

The oedipal myth can be read as one in which a father, out of fear, pushes his son out of his territory, dispossessing the son of his birthright. The son returns and reclaims the territory, including his mother, as his property. Because of his unworthiness as steward (having violated the incest taboo and committed patricide), he is forced to abandon the territory and all he possesses. He retains the affection and care of a daughter, his one last bond, but with his blindness, the possession of power shifts to her.

General agreement holds that however well this myth illuminated male development, it provides a poor guide to female development. The Persephone myth has been chosen by Kulish and Holtzman (1998) as more representative of female development and fantasy during the period from 4 to 6 years old. I believe the Persephone myth not only can, but also must, be read as a metaphoric expression of the dynamics of possession and power. Persephone is abducted by Hades and taken to the underworld to be his consort. Her mother, Demeter, the goddess of grain, comes to Earth to search for her and in her distress creates barrenness and drought on Earth. The gods rule that Persephone may return to Earth and thereby to her mother for a portion of each year, but because she had eaten forbidden pomegranate seeds in the underworld, she must return to Hades and the underworld the remainder of the year. The myth can be interpreted in many ways: a violation of the incest taboo (Hades is Persephone's uncle); Persephone's sexual desire is latent (the active seducer is the man); the mother, Demeter, does not look favorably on men but sees them as dangerous, as rapists; Persephone is caught passively in a state of divided loyalties, but her desire emerges to eat the forbidden seeds—to become pregnant.

Kulish and Holtzman (1998) chose the Persephone myth to be a counterpart for girls to the oedipal myth for boys because they viewed the Persephone myth as indicative of the disavowal of both sexuality and aggression that they regard as characteristic of the oedipal age girl. Although repression of both sexuality and aggression is true of some oedipal age girls, it is not true of others, especially securely attached girls. I believe the Persephone myth's primary message is that the maternal love of mothers who themselves were insecurely attached may take a turn toward the possession of their daughters, both body and mind, and that a man's desire may take the same possessive turn to abduct, kidnap, victimize, and enslave women, at least as seen by the possessive mother. I do not believe such possessiveness by mothers or men is a necessary or universal central dynamic to the development of oedipal age girls, but it is one possible relational pattern and trigger for fantasy.

In romantic love, power is defined by the ability to interest, entice, and seduce, that is, to win over from rivals the object/subject of one's desire. As a result, an oedipal phase child views power in complex ways. A girl knows that her father's charm and good looks excite her; therefore, male charm and good looks have power. She knows that her eagerness to run to Daddy and fuss over him interests and delights him; therefore, female eagerness and admiration have power. She knows that her father's ability to throw and catch a ball, sail boats, and play tennis make her and her mother admire him; therefore, athletic skills have power. She knows that when her mother gets all dressed up in a low-cut gown, wears her best jewelry, and whirls around to show off her new outfit, her figure, and her hairdo, her mother gets her father's excited interest; so, clothes, breasts, accessories, and exhibitionistic flair have power. She knows that when her father tells her mother of a success he has had at work, a promotion and a raise he earned, and a big plan for a vacation, both she and her mother are excited; so, occupational and financial success and opportunities for family play have power. She knows that when her mother tells her father of the cleverness she has shown in her occupational area and her success over a rival, her father enters into a complimentary exchange and delighted looks; so, a woman's wit, competitive skills, and ambitions have power.

What might this oedipal phase girl infer from her observation of what constitutes power? She would recognize that she already has some attributes of power, such as eagerness and other ways to please her father, and she is working to get other attributes of power by taking tennis and sailing lessons. Some attributes she has leave her uncertain whether they give her power or not, such as when people say she has the same dark hair and eyes of her father. Some attributes she cannot have now but will someday (e.g., her mother's breasts, pubic hair, and curves). Some she will never have (e.g., her father's physique and penis). Some she can work to have, such as her mother's or father's occupational skills and ability to function in the big world. In fantasy and symbolic play, she can imagine herself having those attributes that she cannot have, ascribing to her identity whatever qualities of female or male power fit her desires of the moment—a soft and context-sensitive assembly (Harris, 2000) of gender identities.

How does she feel about the attributes of power that she has: proud of those she is working to get, hopeful for those she cannot have, a mix of uncertain possibilities? If starting with a secure attachment, then she has confidence in her own agency and trust in the support of others; she will anticipate the future as providing her with the further attributes for power she will want to have. Consequently, breasts and fancy clothes and mother's adult charm, humor, and cleverness may inspire her admiration. Regardless of her self-confidence, pubic hair and menstruation (and pregnancy) are more complex—inspiring mixes of fear, admiration, and awe. Mother's and father's handling of adult situations of challenge may inspire feelings of idealization, the good feeling of existing under the protective umbrella of competent caretakers. Feeling under a protective umbrella triggers idealization of an adult's attribute whether conceived as masculine or feminine. This type of idealization is without cost to the child; that is, it does not lead her to devalue herself for the absence of the attribute. But, what of the child for whom confidence is less developed because of an insecure attachment or stressful current circumstances?

As confidence wanes, envy, rather than admiration, with all its links to shame, anger, and downcast moods, is the most likely feeling triggered by attributes of power that the child lacks or, because of age limitation, cannot have. Some aspect—say having breasts, having babies, or having a penis—may be selectively idealized in a fashion that the child feels painfully devalued for her lack. Then, envy of the idealized trait along with contempt and disdain for the shame-ridden self will build on social stereotypes of valorizing one gender or the other.

The oedipal phase boy's observations of what has the power to interest, entice, and win out over a rival will follow a basically similar pattern, with specific variations based on ordinary cultural gender biases. Under conditions of secure attachment and a cooperative intersubjectively sensitive family system, the boy's confidence in himself as agent will facilitate his feelings of pride in what he does have; admiration for attributes of both his mother and father; idealization usually of some particular "masculine" trait; and envy of some other attributes, particularly "feminine" body qualities (breasts, womb), empathic sensitivity, and skills. Under favorable circumstances, he will emphasize his skills at "externalities"—action displays to gain "romantic" traction—but not have to sacrifice "internalities" of the ability to listen to and appreciate the point of view of others.

Psychoanalysts have long recognized contexts that interfere with boys having a soft assembly of largely masculine traits along with some feminine traits that help them to feel confidence in their power to interest, entice, and win out over a rival. One such context is the mother who turns to her son to be her little spouse. Whether he absorbs his mother's devaluing or hatred of his father (and men in general) or, without hatred as such, accepts her seduction to relieve her loneliness and despair, the spousified son will feel constrained by what he must give up to achieve his "romantic" victory. The relinquishment of having his masculinity supported by both a father and a mother may lead to intense envy of "phallic" boys who are free of their mother's domination and of girls who (in the child's imagination) can be open lovers of their mothers without heterosexual incest taboo.

Another common context that pushes boys into relinquishments that can lead to intense envy is the situation that arises when the mother is devalued and ineffectual. For the oedipal age son to see his mother treated with contempt and disdain and submissively accept her status, the message is clear to the son: Everything that is like mother is a loser in any test of power. As he exaggerates his macho attributes in actuality and fantasy, he will also unconsciously envy the fantasy of the female who is not so constrained to perpetual heroics, risk taking, and insensitive to self and others.

I cite these examples of contexts that promote problematic envy to contrast them to the many examples in which oedipal age children feel pride in their own attributes, admire attributes they do not have, select some attribute for idealization (and goals for the future), and envy selected others without painful self-devaluation.

The Maturational Influence of a Time Line
of Past, Present, and Future, of an Autobiographic
Organization, and of a Reflective Capacity

What is the ending of the oedipal phase like for children? What problems remain for children entering middle childhood? What gains in development have they obtained? Eagle (2007) challenged the Freudian claim that the source of sexual conflict lies in the inevitable persistence of conflict between incestuous desire and incest taboo. He argued that, although an incest taboo is a universal finding, little evidence supports the universality of pursuing incestuous wishes. Following Mitchell (2002), Eagle recognized an inherent antagonism in adult romantic love between love (attachment intimacy) and desire (sexual lust). Love thrives on security-based familiarity; desire and passion are stirred by diversity, risk, and the excitement of the forbidden. Eagle suggested that a securely attached person could manage the inevitable antagonism of security seeking and excitement seeking without bringing latent incestuous wishes into his or her adult romantic desire. When secure attachment prevails, mates can be chosen who are optimally similar to oneself and one's family members. *Optimally similar* means a compromise between enough dissimilarity to permit sexual feeling without triggering the incest taboo and enough similarity to generate feelings of comfort and safety and formation of an attachment bond.

Because similarity and dissimilarity are in the eyes of the beholder, insecurely attached individuals have biased expectations and perceptions. Enmeshed–preoccupied individuals will experience their partners as too similar to their early attachment figures. Too close similarity results in clinging dependent interactions and deadening of sexual interest based on the carryover of oedipal phase preoccupations. Avoidant–dismissive individuals will experience their partner as dissimilar from early attachment figures, facilitating enactments of detached sexual desire devoid of affection and intimacy.

I would add to Eagle's (2007) proposal that children who are securely attached during the oedipal phase know how as adults to engage partners in an age-appropriate mixture of sensual and sexual desires. In contrast, enmeshed–preoccupied individuals continue to seek some form of sensuality and attachment security with their partners, often under the guise of sexuality. Avoidant–dismissive individuals have essentially abandoned the pleasure and intimacy of sensuality to indulge in the power domination–submission aspect of sexuality as an unconscious substitute for attachment security.

The presumed centrality of the Oedipus complex as integrating all prior development and foreshadowing all later development has come under question from many sources: (a) the significance of attachment strategies as an influence on the manifestations of sensuality and sexuality; (b) indications that oedipal incestuous wishes may not inevitably persist as a source of conflict; (c) the view that castration fears and penis envy are not inherent universals, but when present as full-blown preoccupations are the result of pathological parent–child experiences; (d) the recognition that events, especially traumas at any age, can influence the trajectory of development; and (e) questions from every contemporary analytic theory about the entire hypothesis that a universal buildup of instinctual impulses moves from intrapsychic dyadic representations to triadic representation of psychosexual stages in an autonomous developmental march of solely internal regulation.

Although the claim of centrality has been overstated, I believe oedipal phase relationships are significant, and that some old claims about the oedipal complex remain valid. During the oedipal phase, rather than body sensation pleasure centered on mouth, anus, or skin, genital primacy is established. Children experience their genitals as their most reliable resource for fantasy and soothing sensual pleasures and for sexual fantasy and masturbatory excitement. In addition, as had been recognized, oedipal phase children reorganize their past experience in the light of their current capacities and experiences. The main change in capacity is not experiencing triadic relationships that, as family systems research indicates, has long preceded, but is the ability to place lived experience in a timeframe of past, present, and future in both make-believe play and actuality. A girl's doll's life, a boy's toy soldier's life, whether in imaginative play or in a computer game, has a past and present and moves into the future, creating different perspectives of intentionality. Imagined and real comix into an autobiographic narrative of what we did when we lived in the small house when I was little, how things changed when my brother was born, what mother and I like to do together now, and how proud of me Daddy will be when he sees me swim next week. The history of when we lived in the small house and how things changed when my brother was born will be rewritten from the current perspective of either liking the past better than now or liking now better than then. Although the creation of a more formal autobiographic memory is unique to the 4- to 6-year-old period, the reorganizing of memory is not. Memory will be reflavored, if not reorganized, in adolescence and adulthood and during successful psychoanalysis: Historians say history is rewritten after every conquest.

Children early in life quickly develop implicit knowledge of how to relate in both dyadic and triadic situations. In the experimental design of Fivaz-Depeursinge and Corboz-Warnevy (1999), 3-month-olds playfully engaged with either mother or father will on their own shift their gaze to the other parent momentarily, perhaps to include him or her in the fun or to see if he or she is in sync. In any case, the infants give clear evidence they know the other parent is there. Oedipal age children not only have the same sensitivity to the positioning and perspective of others, but also can construct and hold in mind multiple representations of self with mommy, self with daddy, self with mommy and daddy, daddy with mommy, self alone, mommy alone, daddy alone. The critical factor for the oedipal age child's romantic desires is not simply the multiple representations of being with, but the internal view of the other as that view involves sensuality and sexuality. When Johnny longs for a hug from his mother, what does he find in her eyes, and what does he find in his father's eyes as his mother is hugging him? How much arousal does he sense in his mother as they hug and his body is close to hers? How does what he senses to be in her eyes for him compare to what he sees in her eyes for his father and his father's eyes for her? When Sara climbs into Daddy's lap and snuggles up to him, what does she sense in his body response and his look? Is he welcoming and enjoying, aroused and wary, or aroused and exploitative? What does her mother's look tell her about whether she sanctions and approves or is jealous, hurt, and potentially vindictive? How does what she shares with Daddy compare with what she senses goes on between her father and mother? Stated differently, oedipal age children's desires catapult them into a position as an observer of relationships between their parents and themselves and the parents with each other, while they are themselves the subject of observation by one or both parents. These multiple psychic perspectives foster oedipal age children's capacity to reflect on their own thoughts and feelings and to entertain reflections about the feelings and intentions of others with whom they are interacting, observing, or being observed by.

An optimal ending of children's oedipal phase requires their having developed a capacity for reflective function about the state of mind, the affects and intentions of themselves and others across a broad spectrum of motivations: sensual, sexual, and others. When actual experiences with parents are combined with a child's sense that the intention of the parent of desire is to be fondly and appropriately responsive and the rival parent benignly ironically protective, the child develops a rich fantasy life based on sensual enjoyment and sexual stimulation without fear that his or her sexual desire will be enacted exploitatively or vindictively. Fantasy and reality coexist productively for each. Children can relinquish their desire for actualization of their fantasies, not primarily for fear of punishment, but out of recognition of the wider conceptual reality that encompasses the primacy of the parents' sexual relationship with each other. Their oedipal desires push children into particular curiosity about their parents' general and sexual relationships with each other. From their observations, children are compelled to realize the discrepancy between their physical, conceptual, and sexual immaturity and their parent's physical, conceptual, and sexual maturity. The full implication of the disparity between fantasized maturity and actual immaturity loses its clarity if one or both parents seduce the child into a pseudoadult role as spouse or caretaker. Alternatively, persistent infantilization of the child by one or both parents will cause the child to forfeit the status of a 4- to 6-year-old "romantic player" to be conjured with despite the actual limitations of age.

Children who can take the full measure of their desires, open themselves to fantasy, and hold on to the reality of their limitations vis-à-vis their parents as lovers can take comfort in the realization that once I was little, now I am big enough to express myself sensually and sexually, and someday I will be big enough to do with someone what they do in their bedroom. Children at the end of the oedipal phase can gain confidence in their potential success as wooers in their ability to sense into and evaluate the signs and signals of what and when desires can be expressed based on their maturing capacity for mentalization.

I have described many observations and theories that indicate that children (especially those securely attached and not traumatized by abuse or sexual enactments) can complete the oedipal phase unburdened by the inevitability of conflicts that Freud regarded as universal. Children can complete an oedipal phase having experienced intense oedipal sensual–sexual desires and rivalry without being beset with incestuous wishes, guilt over parenticide, castration terrors, or irresolvable penis envy. As adults, they will have to work with their partner to balance attachment needs for security with the pull for novelty, risk, and excitement. However, no matter how well children leave the oedipal phase, they carry a problem into later years that derives from the socially and culturally cocreated distinction between sanctioned sensuality and the shame-ridden taint of sexuality established early in life. However strongly proscribed, the desire for excitement driven by body pleasure fantasy screams out for expression with a real or imagined partner. The pressure is noticeably strong in the 4- to 6-year-old period, is present but generally less intense during the years before puberty, and then reintensifies. The pressure of sexual desire aroused by bodily craving and fantasy wishes triggered by or searching for external stimulation via human contact or the soft or hard pornography that is ubiquitous is both subversive and transgressive. Sexual arousal and desire have been likened to an itch that will not go away, a mote in the eye, that until tended to clouds all other vision. Stated differently, states of aroused sexual desire can subvert all other intentions and cloud judgments of risk (unwanted pregnancy, AIDS, being caught at marital infidelity, etc.). Aroused sexual desire is transgressive by its nature—that is, the necessity to push against the restraint of childhood shaming (the "Don't do that!")—carried forward in all the don'ts of family, culture, and religion. The heightening of desire supported by peer pressure and the universality of temptations pushes both male and female into the transgressive physical enactments they require to deal with the taboos and mysteries of penetration, menstruation, and pregnancy—all of which lie ahead for the child ending the oedipal phase.

CHAPTER 3

Intimacy With the Gendered Self

INTRODUCTION

By *intimacy with the self,* I refer to a group of experiences that, like most experience, is difficult to put into words. For adults, we can focus on intimacy with the self by asking questions such as what kind of terms are you on with yourself? Do you feel you understand yourself? Are you pleased with the person you are? Do you like yourself as the woman you regard yourself to be—straight, gay, glamorous, feminine, mannish, some of each? Do you like yourself as the man you regard yourself to be—straight, gay, macho, masculine, effeminate, some of each? Do you like yourself as the person others construe you to be?

In their inner speech to themselves, adults carry on a conversation with themselves and often virtual others that bears on all these questions. Compared to outer-directed speech, the inner monologue-dialogue is rapid, imagistic, and less guarded, not withstanding a universal tendency to self-deception. An adult's world of intimacy with the self is largely carried on in inner speech. Psychoanalysis, when successful, taps into this world by creating a sense of intersubjective safety that allows outer verbal and gestural communication to reflect an inner monologue as closely as possible.

Although to some adults intimacy with themselves may seem the quintessential proof of individuation and separateness, contemporary psychoanalysts recognize that from birth one's inner state exists in continuous mutual influence with the affective matrix of others. For the gendered self, intimacy involves not only how one knows and values herself as a female or himself as a male, but also is subject to a consistent mutual influence about herself or himself as seen in the eyes of other women and men.

An adult's intimacy with self is based on higher consciousness: verbal and imagistic symbolization, self-recognition, self-referencing, and reflective awareness of complex constructed and reconstructed maps of self-motives, affects, and relatedness (Edelman, 1992). What of a child prior to symbolic encoding? As the neonate and infant in conjunction with caregivers creates and re-creates maps or categories of repeated events like feedings, diapering, eye contacts, hugs and kisses, awakenings, and sleep cycles, the child develops an experience I can best describe as a sense of familiarity. Familiarity begins a composite lived experience of internal bodily sensation, perception, self in space and interaction, and increasingly defined agency and intentions. A positive feeling of intimacy with one's self builds from frequently repeated good matches between infants' needs and motives and caregiver's responses. Responses highly contributory to a positive sense of familiarity derive from an atmosphere of playfulness that invigorates the ministrations of care (Lichtenberg & Meares, 1996; Meares, 1993; Meares & Lichtenberg, 1995). In the toddler period, play parallel with and then interactively with other children helps to institute a sense of being and having a playmate that becomes a source of liking one's own company in games and as creator of a private world of illusion that often takes on a gender-organized coloration. Play provides an optimal opportunity for learning how minds—one's own and that of others—work. Out of one's companionship with one's mind and body and gender comes self-sympathy and a desire and ability to erect barriers when needed as well as to share with others when guided by love, need, and safety. The junction of self-intimacy and intimacy with others provides a deep sense of internal and external communion that is embedded in our private language, some of which connects the nongendered humanness of everyone and some of which distinguishes male and female intimate expressiveness. A fluid boundary lies between what is regarded as gendered and nongendered humanness because gender provides a plastic flexible receptacle for many characteristics. In our culture, a boy's empathic responsiveness and emotional attunement can be categorized as feminine (Harris, 2000) and a girl's enjoyment of a contact sport as masculine.

OBSERVATIONS OF GENDER DIFFERENCES IN INFANCY

The announcement of "It's a boy!" or "It's a girl!" at birth, with its impact of joy or disappointment, produces an immediate emotional hit for parents and neonate in the period prior to intrauterine gender detection. Now, parents may have adjustment time, but for the newborn his or her gender designation is immediate. Categorical gender identity precedes memory, has no time line in the individual's experience, and is nonnegotiable. The gendered and nongendered symbolized self preexists the child's capacity for verbal representation and self-reference. For infants to cohere their existent and later symbolic sense of self, they must exist already as a symbolic being in a map story in their caregiver's pre- and postbirth expectations. The lived experience of a child with each caregiver evolves from an ongoing negotiation between the individualizing characteristics the infant presents and the parent's expectations based on the symbolic self formed in the parent's mind by the parent's lived experiences. For the gendered self, this last factor assumes great importance. Does the particular infant's biological substrate of size, shape, affects, cuddliness, soothability, and activity level match the caregiver's expectations for a girl or a boy? The developmental path that is crucial for the developing infant and future adult lies in how comfortably the categorical gender identity comes to match its expression as femininity or masculinity in a "soft assembly" (Harris, 2000) with elements of both. In this coconstructed gendered experience, a biological substrate, individual propensities, parental propensities, and cultural pressures play out.

Early gender-specific propensities tend to provide some orientation for differentiating parental responses and confirming or disconfirming parental conscious and unconscious expectations. Sensory responses are generally better organized in girl than in boy newborns. Girls have greater responsiveness to taste, greater mouth activity, and more tongue involvement during feeding, as well as greater overall tactile sensitivity (Korner, 1973, 1974). Thus, a mother may find that the optimal arousal for her girl baby comes with gentler handling, and that the baby responds especially well to oral comforting. The boy neonate's optimal arousal state may require more active handling and jostling or rocking as the mode of comforting. In the fantasies of the parents, these differences easily translate into models of the delicate, sweet (sugar and spice and everything nice) little girl and the rugged, robust little boy. For each parent, his and her gender stereotypes may be satisfying and be affirmed in his or her expectations of the baby or be aversive, leading to tension with the child and between the parents. The inculcation of a feminine identity and role for the girl and a masculine identity and role for the boy continue throughout the first year. Female infants at 12 weeks of age are more sensitive to auditory signals than are boys. Moss (1967) found that girls are talked to more than boys. Females who were touched, vocalized with, smiled at, and played with scored higher on the Bayley Motor Development Test (MDT), whereas boys with actively interactional mothers scored poorer.

Mothers have a greater tendency to maintain physical closeness with 6-month-old girls than with same-age boys (Goldberg & Lewis, 1969). By the end of the first year, masculinity and femininity seem well established in the reciprocal social interplay of infant and family (Fast, 1979). Boys will range farther from the mother and spend less time in actual physical contact with her in free-play situations (Messer & Lewis, 1970). When separated from mother by an artificial barrier, boys are more apt to solve the problem of reuniting by efforts to go around or climb over, whereas girls are more likely to signal distress and a desire to be picked up by crying and raising their arms in a gesture of appeal (Korner, 1974).

Goldberg and Lewis (1969) suggested the following:

> In the first year or two, the parents reinforce those behaviors they consider sex-role appropriate and the child learns these sex-role behaviors … in the same way he learns any appropriate response rewarded by his parents. The young child has little idea as to the rules governing this reinforcement. … As the child becomes older (above age 3), the rules for this class of reinforced behavior become clearer, and he develops internal guides to follow these earlier reinforced rules. (p. 30)

Parens (1979) reported that during the third year a number of observations relating to gender role can be found. Boys begin to be more consistently compelled to push and pull things with their whole bodies, and to crash toys together, than do girls. Both boys and girls of this age more consistently react anxiously to observations of the genitals of the other sex. Parens found that by 3 years of age boys are commonly ready to chase girls, who run away to their mothers, squealing and smiling. At this age, girls, seeing a small baby, will ooh and ahh with delight and express the wish to hold, touch, and feed the infant; boys will often react with indifference.

I regard these behavioral descriptions as informative generalizations about acculturated modalities. These studies fail to tell us about the energetic little boy's fantasies. Especially when he is not so active and is cuddly with his mother, he may imagine that it might be fun to wear lipstick. Or, they do not tell how the running-away, squealing little girl has already decided she wants to be like Daddy in some particular way.

The studies also do not take up the influence of culture on which gendered characteristics are valued and reinforced or devalued and suppressed or the psychological relationship and tensions between parents. They mainly distinguish masculinity and femininity along lines of sensory responsiveness and interactive behaviors.

To what extent can we regard the infant as having a sense of self along gender lines? To have such a sense, the infant would need to know that a distinction of significance exists and be able to integrate his or her own genitals as a crucial representation of the distinction. Persuasive evidence points to the neonate entering a milieu in which male and female others, father and mother in particular, are distinguished early. Brazelton and Als (1979) could tell from 4-week-old infants' actions alone whether the babies were interacting with mother (smoother rhythm) or father (more jerky rhythm). What about the babies themselves? By the beginning of the second year, boys and girls will look longer at photographs of children of the same sex and more quickly put aside pictures of other-sex children (Brooks & Lewis, 1974).

The genital area itself plays an increasingly important role in a developing sense of self. The occurrence of erections and vaginal engorgement from infancy during both rapid eye movement (REM) sleep and awake states indicates that the lived experience contributing to an emerging sense of self includes genital sensation that triggers some level of sensual enjoyment. However, for most infants, sucking and mouthing, rocking and bouncing, and general tactile stimulation are more prominent contributors to the early emergent sense of self. Kleeman's (1975) studies indicate that the genitals are not discovered and explored visually and tactilely in a clearly purposive way until the end of the first year, and that full masturbatory excitement is not consistent until the middle of the second year. Observers of infants tend to agree that between 18 and 24 months, both boys and girls experience an increase in genital and perineal awareness and sensation (Amsterdam & Levitt, 1980; Kleeman, 1975; Roiphe, 1968; Roiphe & Galenson, 1981). This period is a time of great developmental activity and challenge. Greater sphincter control and heightened anal and urethral sensation invite regulatory interactions and struggles. The toddler is increasingly mobile and exploratory and often experiences both exhilaration and anxiety when moving away from caregivers. Growing assertiveness about self-defined goals promotes controversies over opposing agendas with a high potential for intense aversive responses. All of this is given representation by symbolic process augmented by a massive acquisition of vocabulary.

What is the impact of the developments of the 18- to 24-month period on gender, sensuality, and sexuality? First, gender as a designated category is firmly, probably immutably, fixed by this point. Except for highly unusual circumstances, boys are boys and girls are girls, both in the eyes of caregivers and in their own awareness. Second, many aspects of gender behavioral roles are solidly in place. Masculinity and femininity of gesture, movement, and interactional behavior are well established. However, the gender-defining categories do not reveal how many characteristics stereotypically assigned to the other gender (e.g., gentleness or assertiveness, patience or impetuous demanding) are integrated into the emotional/behavior repertoire of a particular boy or girl. Although subject to change at later stages (feminine 2-year-old girls may become tomboys; risk-taking, aggressive boys may become subdued preteens), an overall pattern with many individual variations is established that has lasting significance even if reversed in some particulars in later life.

For both boys and girls, sensual enjoyment is associated with a wide variety of body sensations from the beginning of life. Only gradually do genital-centered sensations assume a prominent role in securing sensual enjoyment and still later sexual excitement. Genital touching, rubbing, and fondling in young toddlers trigger sensual enjoyment and play a prominent role in securing the integration of the genital area into the schema of the body self. The more focused masturbatory activity triggering sexual excitement states of the 18- to 24-month period is responsible for consolidating both image and function of the genital of both sexes into gender designation and gender role. Integrating the genital area into the body schema and the gender designation and role does not tell us what inferences the child draws from his or her recognition. When genital excitement and masturbation activity has been proscribed as shameful, the arousal genital area will be integrated in the body self as different from other body parts—both more evocative and more dangerous. For example, a little boy may at times like and value his penis and the sensations he gets from it. At other times, he might feel that if only he were a girl he would not be scolded and shamed for playing with his penis. Then, his mother would cuddle with him like she does with his little sister and let him be with her more. So, he may stand in front of a mirror and tuck his penis and scrotum between his legs and make believe he is a girl. The boy's fantasy could reflect a fantasy his mother holds for him or a fantasy his father holds for himself. A little girl coming to prize her genital area may devalue it as shameful if in toilet training her mother treats the genital area and anus as inseparably "dirty." From her mother's disgust during cleaning and rough handling, the little girl might infer her genital area is nasty and that she would be better off without it, or she might infer that she would be better served if she had a penis that would be "cleaner." Gilmore (1998) connected toilet training experiences to a cloacae fantasy that accounts for some women's belief that her genital area is dirty and disgusting, and that with sexual stimulation she will lose control and urinate and defecate. A mother who holds such an unconscious belief will transmit it unknowingly to her daughter.

The hypothesis that genital masturbation and sexual excitement contribute to integrating the genital area into a sense of what it means for a boy to have a penis and a girl to have a clitoris, vulva, and vagina has been used to support a phallic-centered view of development. The argument that gender distinction is based on penis possession or penis envy states that, because of the accessibility of the penis and scrotum, the little boy can touch his genital area more readily. Therefore, the male genitals may be easily integrated into the boy's gender identity and role; the girl is incorrectly presumed to be compelled to be aware only of an absence, a deficit, or at best a slit. Kleeman (1975) stated that genital self-stimulation in infant boys "surpassed in intensity, frequency, self-absorption, activity, and precise focusing anything seen in the girls studied" (p. 93). "If you compare the boy's fingering with the use of thigh pressure in the girl, he is registering the sensation in his genitals, his fingers, and his eyes. The sensation in the thighs is less clear and more diffuse" (p. 94). Such a view ignores that the little girl can rub her perineal area to achieve arousal or soothing as effectively as a boy. This view also omits that the little girl's awareness of the potential of her genital area for engorgement, sensual enjoyment, and arousal excitement occurs at ages comparable to those of boys with their penis. Another argument offered is that a boy finds it easier to associate his penis with thrusting than for the little girl to associate her vulva slit and clitoris with reception because she often has no early experience with her vagina or even of its opening (Kestenberg, 1956). This argument implies a failure of imagination that is clearly unwarranted for children, whose fingers explore every crevice and who play "in-and-out" games continuously. Mayer (1995) stated that in the second year girls are aware of and pleased with their genitals and easily capable by cross-modal perception of transforming tactile experience into a visual representation.

A more convincing argument about distinctions between the case of integration by boys and girls of their respective genitals is that the integration may be affected by positive or negative parental response to the toddler's budding sensual expressions. Parents usually name the penis and even the testicles earlier and more accurately than they do the vulva, clitoris, and vagina. Sears, Maccoby, and Levin (1957) document that both boy and girl children frequently deny genital play and masturbation. Moreover, none of the observed parents verbally identified the affective state of either boys or girls during genital play. Both of these failures represent striking "statements" by the parents: They are sending powerful messages to their children. That, as noted in chapter 1, leads to the distinction between acceptable sensual expressions and shameful proscribed sexual expressions. At a time when almost every other activity of the child draws attention, positive or negative, and labeling is a prominent mode of exchange, not to notice, to avert the eyes, or to see and then grow tense and avoidant signals to the child that this activity is "special" in the sense of being beyond the pale. Although parental response to a toddler's genital play is highly individual, observation suggests that in many instances boys' overt displays of sensual activity are more tolerated than those of girls.

Amsterdam and Levitt (1980) noted the shyness and self-consciousness of some toddlers of both genders when viewing themselves in a mirror. The authors speculated that the exchange between the parent and child when the toddler was masturbating or when he or she was proudly exhibiting his or her genital area was responsible for normal or pathological shame-filled self-consciousness. Shaming plays a large role in the later life concerns about penis size, masculinity, and aggressiveness-shyness in males and roundness-thinness, whole body exhibition, and reticence-boldness in females. Thus, shaming affects how comfortable intimacy with the sense of masculinity will be for a boy and the sense of femininity will be for a girl.

Current research no longer supports the theory that the problem for females lies in the anatomy of their genitals. In her "primary sense of femaleness" (Elise, 1997 p. 490), a little girl is apt to be as pleased with her genital area as a boy with his and just as able to form a mental representation of it. The response to the expressions of the boy's maleness and the girl's femaleness will be decisive in the degree of positive affirmation that supports a positive value or shaming impairs loving one's gender. In the past, culture as expressed by parents and carried through intergenerational transmission has not been as supportive of a girl's loving intimacy with her gender as a boy with his.

At various times in psychoanalytic theorizing, either boys or girls have been viewed as having more difficulty consolidating their gender identity. In the discredited phallocentric theory of early psychoanalysis, girls had to cope with their presumed awareness of existence as "deficient" "castrated" males who were made permanently dissatisfied because of penis envy and morally inadequate because of an incomplete superego. Another view gave girls the advantage because they could retain their primary identification with their mother, while boys presumably had to disidentify with their mother to assume a male identity (Greenson, 1966). Much is wrong with these portrayals of development. Healthy mothering builds attachment security and love, not an enmeshment from which neither boys nor girls need to extract themselves.

Fonagy (2001) argued that a boy's secure sense of masculine identity develops from the quality of the boy-to-mother attachment, not their separation. Except for traumatic circumstances, identifications do not overwhelm a passive or helpless child with someone else's qualities. A child capable of agency unconsciously scans his or her whole environment for traits and aspects of others that can be integrated into a cohesive sense of self. An extreme example of this search is the "father hunger" described by Herzog (2001). A powerful unconscious guide to a child's scanning for gendered traits and qualities derives from the conscious and unconscious psychic schema of the boy or girl the mother and father want him or her to be and how each parent "endorses" the masculinity in the boy (D. Diamond & Yeomans, 2007) or the femininity in the girl. In a healthy family system, identifications with any member (mother, father, brother, sister, grandparents, babysitter, etc.) potentially constitute an asset, not a liability. Identification is not a zero-sum game in which having one set of traits means the boy or girl loses or cannot have another. I believe my masculine identity profits from my opportunity to identify not only with the schema of me as "boy" played out with my parents and grandparents but also greatly from identifying with the tenderness, devotion, and affection of the African American women who looked after me throughout my growing up. For both boys and girls, repudiation of opposite-gender traits signals a failure in development and the formation of a defensively rigid masculinity or femininity.

THE RELATIONAL PERSPECTIVE: MUTUALITY OR DOMINANCE-SUBMISSION

In *Bonds of Love* (1988), Jessica Benjamin stated, "The mother's lack of subjectivity, as perceived by both male and female children, creates an internal propensity toward female masochism and male sadism" (p. 81). "Only a mother who feels entitled to be a person in her own right can ever be seen as such by her child, and only such a mother can appreciate and set limits to the inevitable aggression and anxiety that accompany a child's growing independence" (p. 82). In convincing fashion, using the formulation of the failure of mothers to recognize their subjectivity and agency, Benjamin explained both the traditional roles of male dominance and female submission and the extreme forms of sadomasochistic erotic violation. Rather than existence as a passive victim, a woman in Benjamin's view seeks out the idealized male to regain desire and wholeness. While an attempt at active problem solving, a woman's submission to the idealized male is doomed to fail to achieve the goal of a feminine sense of desire and subjectivity in a mutual relationship with a male. Submitting to the male is necessitated by her failure to achieve recognition of her own desire through identification with a mother who herself had a strong sense of her own desire, rather than having been forced to sacrifice her subjectivity.

> The taboo on maternal sexual agency, the defensive mode of separation where the father is used to beat back the mother, the idealization of the father in identifactory love, and the confirmation that dependence and independence are mutually exclusive poles rather than a unified tension—all serve to devalue femininity. (pp. 113–114)

Benjamin thereby hypothesized a transgenerational transmission rendering girls unable to experience desire outside submission. She saw the remedy for this source of dominance–submission vulnerability through the cultural and political revolution of mothers grasping entitlement to be persons in their own right. "The 'real' solution to the dilemma of woman's desire must include a mother who is articulated as a sexual subject, one who expresses her own desire" (p. 114). Assimilating much of what belongs to each parent, the developing girl "could alternatively express herself as I, a woman, I a genderless subject; I, like-a-man" (p. 113).

In broad outline, I find Benjamin's (1988) formulation convincing as an explanation of cultural transmission and useful in understanding clinical problems involving dominance or submission interactions and fantasies, especially when women turn to their fathers and other men for vitality, as illustrated in the case of Veronica in chapter 4. I suggest four modifications of Benjamin's thesis are useful in conceptualizing the path of intimacy with the gendered self.

First, although the development of a little girl's sense of desire is influenced, modified, and shaped by her mother's conscious and unconscious conception of herself and her daughter, the little girl's awareness of desire is not solely dependent on it. The relational-centered view omits the significance of body sensation and the infant's innate motivation for sensual enjoyment. The bodily expression of the motivation for sensual enjoyment unfolds within the intersubjective context of mother–infant, father–infant, and mother–father exchanges. In each intersubjective context, specific pathways to approved-of sensual enjoyment and proscribed sexual excitement result from joint participation in or responses to the child's bodily stimulation. The parental contribution may be playful and accepting, which facilitates a sense of initiative for bodily sensual pleasure, or openly or covertly suppressive and shaming, which constrains initiative. As I described, cultural norms and individual parental proclivities will vary more or less strongly for boy and girl children.

Stating this caveat to Benjamin's formulation differently, a full appreciation of maternal subjectivity requires a focus not only on the mother's recognition of her desire for sexual orgastic excitement but also on the full development of the motivation for sensual enjoyment. Benjamin acknowledged the distinction between sensuality and sexuality when she stated:

> Psychoanalytic valorization of genital sexuality has obscured the equal importance to erotic pleasure of the early attunement and mutual play of infancy. When the sexual self is represented by the sensual capacities of the whole body, when the totality of space between, outside, and within our bodies becomes the site of pleasure, then desire escapes

the borders of the imperial phallus and resides on the shores of endless worlds. (p. 130)

I add that the "imperial phallus" also loses its presumed site as a required focus of desire for erotic pleasure in females when we appreciate the significance for pleasurable and orgastic sensation of panperineal engorgement. Rather than the clitoris-centered miniphallic view of analytic pioneers, perineal engorgement provides the female a full opportunity for an intimate appreciation of her physical and psychological erotic responsiveness (Sherfey, 1966).

A second modification is the distinction between the effect of secure and insecure attachment on the possibility of mother (or father) and child achieving a full appreciation of her (or his) subjectivity and agency. Securely attached children (approximately 60%) have mothers who on the Adult Attachment Interview (AAI; Main 2000) reveal a secure autonomous appreciation of their own attachment experiences, even problematic ones. The mothers (and fathers) retain an ability to call forth a rich recognition of their desires, how they were responded to, and sensitivity to the needs and desires of those with whom they have been intimate. Although the AAI reveals a mother's appreciation of attachment experience but not of the subjective awareness of sensual or sexual desire or of gendered issues of domination and submission, I believe we can make tentative extrapolations to sensual–sexual motivations. Secure autonomous women, I suggest, are likely to be open to subjective awareness of their desire for sensual enjoyment shared with their children and adult partner and for sexual excitement not shared interactionally with their children but sought and shared with an adult partner. If society pressures them to accept roles of female submission, then they can make that adaptation without essential loss of themselves as an agent of desire. If societal pressures change (and they may be useful proponents of societal change), then they are apt to have the flexibility to comfortably move into roles of mutuality and reciprocity. Thus, for 60% of mothers and their children, we can expect them to be open to an intimacy with others and with themselves that reflects both nongendered and gendered desires and openness to mutuality. These autonomous mothers and secure daughters are apt to have the flexibility to experience themselves as "I, a woman; I, a genderless subject; I, like-a-man" (Benjamin, 1988, p. 113).

An additional perspective derives from a comparison of forms of insecure attachment. Avoidant and anxious resistant attachment of children and their adult counterparts in dismissive and preoccupied patterns of behavior and communication can easily be related to impaired appreciation of the subjectivity of self and others and to domination–submission themes in action and fantasy. The avoidant infant and dismissive adult turn away from or are dismissive of the approach and inner desires of others with whom intimacy might be possible. As children or adults, they are not unaware of the intent of others, but through limiting their own affects, avoiding commitment, and turning contact into rituals, they remain insensitive to the subjectivity of others and themselves. Refusal to listen to, care deeply about, or sense into the feelings of others is a form of controlling or dominating a relationship. In its sexual form, insensitivity to the feeling of a partner turns lovemaking into a controlled and controlling form—often accompanied by domination fantasies. Not to listen to or care about the feelings of a partner while acting possessively is commonly stereotyped as male, as in the "men are from Mars" cliché, but it occurs in both men and woman with avoidant attachments.

In contrast, anxious ambivalent children and preoccupied adults are so caught up with their inability to reconcile their wishes with those of others that they become slaves to their hyperinvolvement. However much their preoccupied attachment may resemble intimacy, they cannot create the open space with their partners they would need to appreciate the individuality of either self or other. Their reading of the desires of the other is skewed by the centrality of their need to obtain attuned resonance with their wishes from others. They cannot tolerate uncertainty or ambiguity sufficiently to appreciate the fluctuating convergence and divergence of self-interest in each member of a dyad. A common pattern in their relationships is an attempt to gain continuous involvement and reassurance (a form of domination) through clinging, shadowing, and surrender of initiative (a form of submission). At times, they take on the role of devoted altruistic caregiver-slave. In its common gendered form, anxious–ambivalent children become playground victims (crybaby girls and sissy boys), and preoccupied adults become masochistic surrenderers to an expected exploitation. In gendered stereotypes, adults who ineffectually plead for sensual–sexual response from their partner or who surrender to the pace, appetites, and preferences of the other are regarded as "feminized" in the view of self or other whether the gender identity is male or female.

The sensual–sexual patterns of both avoidant–dismissive and preoccupied adults incline them toward domination–submissive behaviors and fantasies and away from mutuality with their partners. However, these are not the attachment disturbances that are most likely to lead to the more serious erotic enactments. Seeking arousal through participation in experiences of inflictor or victim of pain, abuse, degradation, or drug-induced altered states is more likely associated with disorganized–disoriented infant and unresolved disorganized adult attachment. These children experience moments of confusion, even dissociation, during which they appear to lose any sense of organized agency. The research indicates that many of these children are victims of physical and sexual abuse. Others have been subjected to episodes during which their parents have been frightened or frightening. When the caregiver a child seeks for security is herself (or himself) a source of inexplicable and unpredictable anxiety or actual danger, the child is caught in an irresolvable dilemma between approach and withdrawal. Other experiences that trigger similar irresolvable dilemmas involve excessive shaming, confusing submission on the part of parents to the infant's aggression, or sexually overstimulating behavior such as deep kissing, exhibitionism, or encouragement of genital caressing (Hesse & Main, 1999).

Adults who during childhood have suffered these irresolvable traumas experience confusion, disorganized reasoning, and dissociation in response to their memories or current reactivations. Those disorganizing experiences interfere with an appreciation of subjectivity, the person's own or others, across a broad spectrum of motivation. Rather than attentive to the feelings and desires of another person, they may tend toward intensified negative affect states, hypervigilance, and self-centeredness. Alternatively, they may be subject to dissociation with affective deadening, fog states, and robotlike behaviors. In either case, cognition is impaired and reflective awareness nonexistent. The relationship of unresolved trauma and disorganized attachment to borderline and dissociative states has been well documented; the relationship to sexual enactments is more conjectural.

Psychoanalysis long ago pointed to overstimulation. More recently, an astonishing frequency of overt sexual seduction and abuse of children has come to light. The profound sense of distrust of others and debasement of the self, especially when the seducer-abuser is also a person to whom the child has an attachment contributes to addictive playing out of eroticized domination–submission themes.

The overstimulated hyperarousal states tend to obscure the equally profound disruption that results from a deficit of sustaining empathic sensual experiences. Children and adults coping with the deadening effect of sensual understimulation and affective dissociation will seek enlivening in a variety of forms: pain as a stimulant to body awareness, rage and destructiveness, fire setting, drug highs and lows, pornography, and a wide variety of domination–submission sexual schema that may combine any of these elements. In the schemas, sometimes in behavior, always in fantasy, the roles are fluid regarding perpetrator-victim, masculine-feminine in changing combinations. Although these erotic practices are fluid in accompanying fantasies, the individuals in their conscious awareness of self are often rigidly polarized as tough guy supermales and dominatrix females or subservient mousy women and limp-wristed feminized males, although many variants of other rigid gendered identities exist. Adults who are unresolved with respect to domination traumas struggle with the need to regulate sensual sensation and sexual arousal in repetitive rigid form that freezes them to live in a self-centered world of immediacy. Their world lacks perspective about their own desires and the enactments they are drawn for engagement. Their world lacks perspective also about the desires and subjectivity of others, who exist only to serve the function of immediate regulation of a disturbed affect state. Locked in a here-and-now world of limited consciousness, they press themselves and others to engage in scenarios of lustful indulgence without any opening to higher consciousness of past and future and the reflective awareness that opens to possible change.

My final comment on Benjamin's (1988) formulation of the origin of female domination–submission patterns is that the focus on the lack of subjectivity in the mother can be expanded to any pairing that is significant during a child's development. In families in which a father has had his agency subverted and his sexual and other desires treated with contempt, the likelihood of master–slave relatedness is great for both male and female children. The overt and covert roles will vary greatly, some culturally played out as in many matro-dominant societies or social groups. The introduction into a child's life of the deleterious effect of subjectivity is not dismissed, ignored, or obliterated, confined to the parental pairing. In many multigenerational homes or clans, the conspiratorial playing out of dominant and submissive factions (Serbs and Bosnians) or the quarantining or alienation of individuals (HIV victims) is unfortunately not uncommon. In my clinical experience, a particularly frequent source of pervasive domination–submissive fantasies and sexual schemas lies in sibling emotional, physical, and sexual abuse. The tantalizing mixture of omnipresent playmate, competitive rival, and available "object" on whom to enact a panoply of emotional desires and trauma-derived affects creates a love–hate interplay that often characterizes later attachment and sexual relatedness. The covert umbrella of parental denial that permits a child to abuse his or her sibling gives to the abuser a sense of affirming complicity and to the victim a sense of unprotected helplessness (see Lichtenberg, Lachmann, and Fosshage's 1996 volume, *Clinical Exchange,* for an example of maternally "sanctioned" sibling sexual abuse).

Returning to intimacy with the gendered self, Benjamin's study points to the principal process that facilitates the growth of all intimacy with the self: a full appreciation of one's own subjectivity and the capacity to appreciate the subjectivity of another. In psychoanalysis, four explorations intertwine to promote intimacy with the gendered self:

1. Can I as analyst open myself in the presence of this analysand to empathically sense into my responses, reflect on them, and have a flexible evolving mental picture of me with her or him?
2. Can I as analyst help the analysand to open him- or herself to sense into deepest private experiences, reflect on them, and develop a flexible evolving picture of him- or herself with others and with me and thereby enable this person to build an increasing sense of agency, of existence as a center of initiative?
3. Can I as analyst open myself to the masculine and feminine feelings and role responses triggered by my female or male patients' sensual and sexual associations and initiatives?
4. Can I as analyst help this person to open him- or herself to recognize, appreciate, and accept sensual and sexual desires as these desires arise, sometimes unequivocally heterosexual, sometimes unequivocally homosexual, often mixed and confused and invariably more nuanced than categoric?

The soft assembly of gender roles, behaviors, and more significantly fantasies and unconsciously activated responses applies to both analyst and analysand. Intimacy regarding the gendered self in psychoanalysis is a dyadic coconstruction.

CHAPTER 4

Veronica

A Clinical Example of Achieving Intimacy With the Gendered Self

INTRODUCTION

Veronica was on her way home from graduate school during a holiday when her car broke down. With trepidation, she called her father, who, as she expected whenever anything made him anxious, railed at her: "How can you be so stupid that you can't look after your car properly?" Shattered, she went into her robot fog state, which lasted through the whole vacation period. She arranged to see the counselor who had helped her through high school and college. The contacts had been intermittent, depending on the severity of Veronica's bulimia. Her treatment could never be called psychotherapy; for Veronica and her family, the euphemism of counseling was more acceptable. On this occasion, the level of concern of both therapist and Veronica rose to the point at which a more consistent treatment was agreed on and she was referred to me.

The fog state having lifted, Veronica struck me as an attractive, vibrant, almost hypomanic, ambitious, resourceful, bright young woman. From her prior therapy, she had formed a picture of her family that she could readily relate. Her father, a successful industrialist, dominated the family. He was easily made anxious whenever anything threatened his control, and he had frequent temper outbursts. Her mother, who possessively doted on Veronica, was completely submissive to her husband's demands. Veronica had grown up in an affluent suburb, was a successful athlete in several sports, and was at the top of her class as a conscientious, dedicated student. Her friendships with females were heavily tinged with rivalry. Throughout high school, college, and graduate school, she dated, although as far as I could tell she had never been really close with any male.

A symptom that presented early in the treatment was nighttime panics. She could not calm herself enough to get to sleep. She used alcohol and cigarettes to produce a fog state, finally getting to sleep, only to be disturbed by upsetting dreams of disasters. Her family visited and for several days enjoyed the sights of Washington, D.C. Then, on returning to their hotel, she became confused momentarily about directions. Triggered by this trivial disruption, her father erupted, screaming at her in the middle of the street. Her mother stood helplessly by, later comforting Veronica with her oft-used phrase, "Your father doesn't mean it; he loves you." An understanding of the attachment, nonerotic aspect of Veronica's fog states and nighttime disturbance unfolded over a period of time. In the D-category paradigm proposed by Hesse and Main (1999), Veronica's father was both frightened and frightening (also shaming and seductive). In the middle of the night, if a thunder-and-lightning storm occurred, he would awaken the whole family in a state of great anxiety, insisting they all go to the basement and hover together. As Veronica got older, she no longer believed in her father's reasons for panic at storms but could not help but be caught up in his frightened state. Her father's frightener side lay in his raging and screaming. In a caricature-like style of an adult temper tantrum, at his club he would break up golf clubs or slam tennis rackets. The other men would laugh at him, but he was fully accepted in the country club life. Veronica could disavow her embarrassment at her father's public displays of temper when they did not involve her. However, his screaming at her at home in front of her friends or the sound of his voice criticizing her and heard above the cheers and hoots of other parents during athletic events would resonate in her ears for hours. As soon as she could be alone, she would walk outside, smoke, look at nature, and enter a dissociative state. Her mother, ever alert to when Veronica was not her smiling, effervescent "self," would cajole her to forgive her father and forget what he had done because "he didn't mean it." Veronica was sent to calm him so peace would be restored, and he would not take out his anger on her mother.

A model scene that we used frequently occurred in a small sailboat he bought her after she had come home from camp and mentioned having learned to sail. He insisted on going out on the lake with her. She was in fact unskilled, and as the boat wavered out of control, he panicked and began screaming at her. She dissociated and somehow robotlike got them to shore. In some renderings of this scene, she would emphasize her appreciation of his giving her anything she wanted; in others, she would emphasize more her outrage at his panicked screaming at her, the love–hate theme giving the model scene its organizing principle.

The first of the three romantic attachments that became central to analyzing her sensual–sexual problems occurred during her last year of graduate school and continued over a 2-year period. Jerome was a free spirit with an exotic background who attended class irregularly but still made good grades. His star quality appealed to Veronica, who was a conscientious, ambitious, hard worker who valued academic skills. Soon after they started going together, in a session that challenged my Eew! factor, Veronica told me with glowing excitement that Jerome had stayed with her all night after she had agreed to have sex. Her way of announcing the event and the evasiveness that followed made me uneasy.

I inquired about the details of her experience, and with offhand bravado, Veronica said he came in her, and it was great because she had nothing to cause her to worry.

Analyst: What do you mean, nothing to worry about?
Patient: He was on top from the back.
A (tone rising): From the back?
P: Yes, my backside, that's what made it safe.
A (same rising tone): Safe?
P: Yes (defensively). I couldn't get pregnant. What are you upset about? I got him to stay with me!
A (my revulsion still strong): I don't consider anal penetration a loving act of a man being respectful to you.
P: Well I had to do it that way.

Veronica's tone was both defiant and pleading. By now, I was beginning to regain my composure. I realized my outburst of disgust and disdain was triggered by revulsion at "buggering" but was set up by latent distress at my inability to help her manage her addictive pattern of placing herself in situations of "disrespect"—one that we were now enacting between us. Now calmer, I picked up the tone of desperateness in her statement: "I had to do it that way." We began an inquiry that opened up the persistence of her childhood fear of pregnancy from any contact with a male. She had accepted the teaching that kissing, touching genitals, or contact of any sort with secretions could lead to pregnancy and the worst possible disgrace.

Veronica was in a state of first love and anguish. Jerome treated her with total casualness. He would make no arrangements to formalize getting together. After a night together, he would parade in front of her with another girl, his rumored fiancée. Jerome became a spectral figure over the next 2 years. He might appear wherever she was or suddenly call and inquire about her. She would track him when she could and with each "sighting" become full of anguish. By now, she was meeting and becoming friendly with many other men. She was contemptuous of those who behaved submissively toward her as she did with Jerome, finding their infatuation with her clingy and smothering like her mother's. Following Benjamin's (1988) formulation, Jerome had become the ideal man, the source of desire and agency. He felt entitled to dominate and operate freely on his will alone with no consideration of the feelings of the other.

Finally, ephemeral Jerome disappeared entirely, to be replaced by Carlos. Carlos was a male star of the athletic team for which Veronica was a female star. The other woman players advised Veronica that Carlos was bad news, a man who used women and could never make a commitment. Carlos and Veronica began prancing in front of one another and quickly their affair took form. He might go home with her after their athletic events, but she could never know in advance or count on it. Once together, they might have intercourse, and he might stay or leave. She might refuse as an expression of her anger and then become the aggressive tantalizing seducer. She desperately wanted him to accompany her to an office party but was too hesitant to ask him. As I explored her severe anxiety, probably more to shut me up than out of conviction she asked him to go to the party, and as she expected and feared, he refused. She threw a party for their mutual friends, asking him to come early. She waited all evening, painfully aware of her embarrassment. By 2 a.m., everyone had left except for two of her male friends, who helped her to clean up. At 3 a.m., Carlos appeared with an excuse they both knew was meaningless. Torn between her outrage and her relief and eagerness to see him, she let him stay. After this, she determined to break with him, and a painful period followed.

She became obsessively preoccupied: Would he call or come over, should she call him? Would he acknowledge her presence at athletic events or ignore her? As the intervals between nighttime contacts lengthened, she became increasingly despondent. She would enter the office with her eyes averted and slumped posture and would have long periods of silence. I would time my comments and questions to some movement on her part. She began to attack me with increasing intensity. I was the cause of her misery. Didn't I know how much she needed him? Her nightmares were terrible. Only his call or coming over could make the fog she lived in go away. She was drinking herself to sleep. Didn't I worry about her drinking and her feeling she couldn't go on? I assured her I did worry. I arranged for Klonopin for sleep, offered her extra hours of therapy, had her have telephone sessions when I was away, and always let her know where I would be on weekends. She would call when she needed but never abused the arrangement.

During the sessions, I focused my inquiry on her belief that only his coming to her would bring her out of the fog. She revealed that after terrible bouts with her father she would retreat to her room completely undone. He would come to her. He would tell her he did not mean his outburst; it was just the pressure of his work. He would cajole her to forget what happened. He would call her seductively by his pet name for her, "Nica, Nica, Nica, come smile at me," until she would melt and smile, and they would embrace. This revelation did little to change the impasse. Moreover, further pain came from her situation at work, where the chief executive officer was leaving her out and showering attention on people she regarded as sucking up to him. Her pride would not let her play the sycophant, and she began her shunning "I won't come to you, you come to me" behavior with him. Now, jealousy became a more pronounced theme. She railed contemptuously at the women at work who this executive favored, at the women to whom Carlos talked, and at my wife, who lived stuck with me in a conventional world that Veronica demeaned and to which she would never belong. As her hatred mounted and with it the viciousness of her attacks on me, I tried to remain steady, noting to her that she was letting herself begin to recognize a side of herself she had never acknowledged. She not only was the gay, brilliant young woman on top of the world or the poor sad victim of abusive unreliable men but also was capable of hatred and vengeance. She added, "Like my father." During this time, her appearance changed, her face broke out, and her previously impeccable clothing became sloppy, with runs in her hose. During one sustained attack, feelings within me welled up, and I shouted back: "OK, do you really want to fight? If you do, I can fight, too!" Her demeanor changed. She became calmer and said she felt the fog had lifted. This exchange between us did little to alter her preoccupation with Carlos, but it did lessen her attacks on me.

The next crisis again involved a car. Veronica came in completely distraught and told me she had to go home for a holiday because her mother had sent her tickets, saying: "Your father misses you so much." On inquiry, Veronica said she could neither refuse nor go. The principal horror was that her father would insist they go to visit his mother. It was a long drive; he would be tense about seeing his mother, who neither he nor anyone in the family liked. Something always happened on the road, and he would start screaming at her mother or her, and she would be frozen, trapped in the car for hours. What should she do? As usual, I was no help. I suggested that she had to choose not going home—Veronica interrupted: "I have to, I can't just not see them. They are my family"—or negotiate a plan that would make it safe for her. Veronica, interested, asked, "Like what?" I responded, "Like not doing what you don't want—visiting your grandmother—and picking out things you do want, like seeing your friends." The effect of this exchange was like glass shattering. Veronica emerged from her fog with a burst of purposeful agency. She called her parents, who accepted her parameters, and the visit went well. She also changed jobs, going to a company where she worked under two successful women she liked. Going to work under competent women represented Veronica's attempt to derive vitality and agency from women rather than from narcissistic men.

Veronica's contact with Carlos was now limited. She tried to set conditions that he assured her he would not meet. She tried to make him jealous by dating a friend of his. Her attempt was to no avail, and the affair began to peter out. The next crisis was directly with her father and again involved a car. Her parents came to visit her, and she planned a number of activities. She felt that if she took charge more actively, the situation would go better because at any uncertainty her father became anxious. She was driving on a familiar route, but one in which a mistake is easy to make, and she made a wrong turn, possibly as a result of anticipatory tension. Her father said something, she did not remember quite what, and she froze. She pulled over, slowly recovered enough to drive robotlike to their destination. When they came out of the restaurant, she handed her father her car keys, saying, "You drive. I can't." Subsequently, believing her concentration was adversely affected, Veronica worried that she was losing her credibility at work and had a full return of insomnia, drinking nightly, and disaster nightmares. After work, she was holing up in her apartment, not contacting friends, and even forgoing the athletic events that had sustained her in the past. The car experience I believed had triggered a serious traumatic dissociative state of altered consciousness. We increased the frequency of meetings, and I urged Veronica to reenter her trancelike state in the car while with me. She filled in detail after detail as we relived the experience together. Furthermore, we were more successful than before in relating the content of the persistent nightmares to the traumatic effect of daytime experiences. We were able to integrate our understanding of the recent experience in the car with the model scene work we had done with the original car breakdown and the rejected car trip to see her father's mother. We could contrast the sense of helpless victimization in the first and third episodes with the sense of agency when she "had her voice" in the second episode. She began to recognize that she would lose her voice not only when frightened by her father's anger or his anxiety but, also, when in her postabuse fog state, she would welcome seduction as a restorative. Seeing the abuser–seducer pattern with her father helped to integrate the experiences with Jerome and Carlos.

In the recovery of the memory of the recent car episode, the passive ineffectual role of her mother became more directly illuminated than before. Although she went along comfortably with our recognition of her father's part, she bridled at looking at her mother's role, screaming at me, "Are you going to take everything away from me?" I acknowledged the significance of her attachment to her mother, but she and I both knew that her mother's failure to protect her, even pushing her back to soothe her father, was a component of the problem. As she calmed, we could go further and integrate the feelings about her mother's failure with her oft-repeated criticism of me for not protecting her.

After our analysis of the traumatic dissociative episode in the car, Veronica's spirits improved and with it her appearance. At work, she regained her enthusiasm and ambition. In the evenings, her loneliness began again, and her complaints echoed her charge to me that I had taken everyone away from her. She would never have a mate. Her friends were all now married, and several had children. My conventional submissive wife had conventional male me. Her friends and my wife could marry because they could play the submissive catering role of her mother. I had shown her that she was not really like that. She was loud and raucous, a competitive athlete. If I had helped her find her voice, then I had shown her she was the type of woman no man would want. I assured her I did not share her pessimism, and that many men preferred mutuality and reciprocity in their relations. She admitted she knew of some such arrangements. She cited a cousin who was married to a successful Jewish professional woman the family criticized. Although her criticism remained, a subtle change occurred in her attitude toward me. The "you" she now used when speaking to me seemed to give me a personhood—like the difference in French between *tu* and *vous*. Before I was a counselor, a hired hand she used to serve her needs. Now, she might say, "I don't have anyone I feel close to but you" or "I know I can tell you even if I don't feel like confiding in anyone." And then, Dick appeared.

Dick was the youngest member of senior management. Veronica showed interest in an after-work project he had, and he offered to mentor her. After their work, they would go for a drink to discuss their plans. Gradually, the conversation turned more personal, and Veronica detected that despite his seriousness about the project, he was taken with her. She became anxious and restless with preoccupations of "Will he? Won't he?" Did he need encouragement, or was she deluding herself? Then, he made clear his infatuation with her, and she was joyous. Here was a man she could respect who was considerate of her wishes and thoughtful in his responses. He was a man she could marry. She did not want to tell her mother yet. Her mother would start bragging to everyone and talk to Veronica about nothing other than Dick and Veronica's mission to hold on to him. A flicker of doubt began when Veronica stayed at Dick's apartment for the first time. After much enjoyable foreplay, he did not complete intercourse because he had no condoms. Although she did not want to, she could not stop comparing him with Carlos. With Carlos, sex had been awesome, wild and free. Maybe Dick was not man enough. After a weekend trip, this worry passed, only to be replaced by another. Dick asked her if she had been smoking, and she denied it. To my inquiry, she replied she did not want to lose him. I responded that she was in danger of losing herself if she did not feel the person he cared about was the person she knew she was. Furiously, Veronica asked whether I wanted her to tell him she smoked and drank herself to sleep. He kept telling her she was wonderful. If I caused her to lose him, she would quit me forever.

In subsequent hours, Veronica was distressed but with a difference. She did not dissociate into a fog state with eye aversion and silence. She now addressed me in a direct confrontational manner that had not been there before. Increasingly uncertain of herself with Dick, she turned to her mother for advice. Her mother eagerly recommended her program for how to get and hold a man. Be nice, cater to his whims, do not wear clothing that reveals her legs because they are her least-attractive feature, and invite Dick to the family ski lodge. Veronica mulled this over, fumed at me, and went in and out of her fog state. Out, she was feeling resentment in all directions: at her female seniors at work, at me, and increasingly at Dick for his workaholic hours, so like her father's. In the fog, she was attempting to play out the role with him that her mother had laid out for her. She began to yearn for Carlos. She felt bereft, and a nocturnal visit from Carlos would bring her out of the fog. Then, she received a huge boost when very important senior people in her industry invited her to serve on a prestigious committee. Buoyed by this recognition, she made an unusually frank assessment of her strengths in integrating information and making a favorable impression on people and her weaknesses, the technical areas in which her knowledge was limited. Returning to the stalled issue with Dick, she described a situation in which he had failed to let her know he would be unavailable. She thought he might be afraid to upset her. I suggested that maybe they were both afraid to have the other know them as they were. Really knowing one was a necessary step to begin the negotiating and adjusting that they needed to have their relationship become one of mutual concern for the other. Her wariness returned but without her appearing to dissociate into lessened contact with me. I added that I knew she was afraid of what might happen if he lost his idealized view of her and she of him.

The next hour she reported that over the weekend they had had several long talks, and it was good. She told him about her feelings about his work keeping him away from her, and he told her about the ambitious projects he had and his strong investment in them. Nonetheless, he assured her of his love for her and his expectation that they could work it out; she felt better. Glaring at me, she said, "I trust him more than I trust you." I answered, "His assurance made you feel safe, and my urging you to openness put you at risk." She nodded, and the hour moved into an exploration of the problems of "having a voice." She was happy now, but wondered what would happen if he dropped her. She felt he could anytime if he did not like something she said or did. I picked up on her doubts about two people respecting each other's interests—often convergent, sometimes divergent. She ended the hour with the reflection that she had noticed her mother and father were getting along better, and that her mother was becoming outspoken in taking up for herself.

In the ensuing period, Veronica vacillated between a sense of secure attachment to Dick and anxiety triggered by anything that linked him to her father's patterns of avoidance through work or his anger. The difference lay in her response to the upset periods. She could place the experiences in a larger context that helped her to unfreeze. We would talk about the events with an openness to a give-and-take interaction previously impossible. Her dreams reflected her increased ability to regulate her affect. Rather than nightmares, they were more conventional anxiety dreams, such as a dream in which others were able to complete a trip to Niagara Falls (meaning marriage) while she was left behind. Her approach to the relationship with Dick was more sober and grounded in an intention to try to work out problems as between equals and peers.

Unfortunately for Veronica, her progress was not mirrored by Dick, who unexpectedly for her (and me) not only dropped her but also refused even to make eye contact or acknowledge her presence when they met in professional settings. Veronica went into an emotional funk characterized by insomnia, anxiety, anger at me, and an intense, almost delusional, insistence that Dick must come back, must call her. Nothing I could say or offer helped, and reiterating what we knew of her father's "making up" charm episodes fell flat. Something in Veronica's tone, a little girl voice as she insisted he must come back, triggered my conjecture that Veronica was dealing with a vulnerability other than the oedipal configuration with her father, a vulnerability derived from an earlier (or at least different) source. Veronica's stock portrayal of her mother was that she was always seeking Veronica out for company and solace, for stories to brag about to her friends, and to shower Veronica with gifts and clothing as though she were a Barbie doll. This view was well substantiated by current experiences. Spontaneously, I asked Veronica about her mother's diabetes. She responded that when she was small her mother had great difficulty getting her diabetes under control, and that her father's outbursts would make it worse. Veronica responded to this line of inquiry with interest and an affective shift. Together, we developed the picture of Veronica's mother having episodes of physiologically induced discontinuities that were inexplicable to the little girl. The "he" of "he must come back," "he must call" served to obscure the symbolic condensation of the abandoner: she (of the need for a secure base attachment) and he (of oedipal desire) must return to reestablish sustaining affective connection.

An unexpected sequence of events followed. On a driving trip with her family through the Southwest, Veronica, rather than ineffectually ridiculing her father with other family members, directly confronted him. She declared that his temper outbursts, harangues, and road rage behaviors were unacceptable. If he did not agree to stop, then she would fly back to Washington. Despite the absence of support from other family members, Veronica remained firm, and they completed the trip.

On her return, Veronica switched employment to a prestigious position that required retraining and working in a competitive environment. Now, having the voice she had found in challenging her father, she was more effective at work despite brief periods of depressive anxiety when she was "out of favor." Many of Veronica's upsets were triggered by her intense competitiveness and the rivalries she entered. If she wished to cultivate a male boss and another female equally bright but more willing to be openly seductive was more successful than she, then she would rant at me that she would not demean herself to make up to a man. Likewise, if she wished to be recognized as superior to a male competitor and other males did not acknowledge her, then she would rant to me about old boy's clubs and their exclusionary practices. She was also at odds with her childhood and school friends, all now married and having children, subjects that dominated their conversations with her. While she poured out her anger to me, her actual behavioral strategy was to be compliant and submissive when challenged and sulky and avoidant otherwise. I pointed out to her that although I could easily appreciate her hurt and anger at exclusion, the efforts she made to gain the inclusion and recognition she wanted and often deserved were ineffectual and counterproductive. Veronica reported a vivid dream that upset her. She suddenly saw a tornado approaching; no, she said, it was two tornados. She was terrified but saw a building that she was able to find a way to get under to take refuge, and then she woke up. We had long before identified the tornado as a reference to her father's temper and to his fear of actual tornados, cowering in the basement with the whole family during storms. As Veronica described the building under which she took refuge, we both recognized it as standing for my office, which is on a lower floor of my house. Veronica generally did not like to acknowledge openly the protection she felt from me, but she asked: "Two tornados?" I answered: "The second one is you. You have a temper like your father. You have as much power as he but you don't know yet how to harness it to get what you want." Not long after this session, Veronica conceptualized a project at work that required much diligence and skilled interpersonal maneuvering. The success of the project was reported in newspapers and won her awards.

Around this time she mentioned to Anthony, a professional at her level in a different department, that she planned a vacation trip, and he asked to go along. This led to pleasant contacts, sealed by another more extensive trip. Thus began the romance that led to marriage, a romance characterized by its lack of drama. Anthony came from a less-affluent, less-prestigious, lower socioethnic family; was reliable, caring, unintrusive, competent, and steadfast, all positive attributes that were on the other side of the coin of her transferential ridicule of "dull conventional me and my conventional wife." Veronica knew Anthony was not going to be the prize her mother wanted her to bring home, but she was nonetheless determined to persist. Battles flared about the wedding and the church, with her mother becoming suddenly helpless and trying to consult Veronica continuously. Veronica refused to leave her work project to come to her parent's home weeks before the wedding so her mother could entangle her further into both her pseudohelplessness and a social whirl. Then, she refused to let her mother accompany her to the final fitting for her wedding dress, and her mother went into a 2-day withdrawal sulk. Supported by Anthony, Veronica refused to succumb to the guilt inducement, and peace was restored. Her mother appeared to recognize that she was now dealing with a different Veronica, a Veronica who knew what she wanted for herself and would fight to get it.

We continued treatment sessions with reduced frequency as Veronica's career flourished based on her hard work, dedication, and creativity. Veronica and Anthony decided they wanted to have a child, and then she faced a minicrisis about her smoking and drinking. Veronica, now in her mid-30s, had since her teen years used smoking, drinking, and dissociating as a way to regulate her tension and to allow herself to go to sleep. The implicit understanding we arrived at was that she understood the risk to the child and would act accordingly in her own way in her own time. She resented her mother's fluttering over her with anxious comments. For my part in our implicit agreement, I contained my anxiety, not so much about whether she would rein in her smoking and drinking but how disrupted she would be without it. And, first smoking and then drinking ended, with Anthony and me cheering her on after the fact.

Veronica then became pregnant. Her mother now panicked that she should watch her weight or she would never be able to lose it. Veronica was working on a second major project. The project and fending off her mother's intrusions were all she talked about for the first 6 months. She described her mother as subjecting her to Chinese water torture of continuous little digs about her weight, her housekeeping, and Anthony's relaxed (supposedly unambitious) habits. I expressed my curiosity about thoughts about the baby, perhaps a name. Sensing my anxiety about her preparedness (a mother transference), Veronica assured me that when the time came she would know all she needed to know about delivery, breast-feeding, nipple care, schedules, and whatever. She had the good fortune that a woman she was partnering with on the project had also become pregnant at the same time, and they confided in each other. She felt well prepared for maternal feelings based on her care for her two dogs; she fretted over, played with, walked with, and worried about them when she had to be away, believing no one but she looked after them properly. This recitation of maternal preoccupation was in keeping with the core theme of the beginning of the end of Veronica's analysis. She was telling me, "I know what I want, and I know how to go about getting it. I like support—yours and Anthony's and my pregnant professional partner's—but I do what I need to on my own schedule." I heard Veronica telling me to trust her as neither of her parents could, and that she would do fine when she could; when she could not, she knew how to get what she needed from me.

Veronica juggled baby care while keeping track (and control) of her project from home. We kept sessions going by phone until Veronica brought her baby in for my admiration and delight. He has the same up-tempo energetic proclivities as Veronica. Veronica expressed admiration for Anthony's unfailing support and disdain for his inability to calm the baby the way only she (the mother) could.

We appeared to be on schedule for setting an ending date. Veronica was developing her major project while reiterating her complaint that she was not one of the guys who went out for drinks together after work, and she felt isolated. She also complained that she was unappreciated, a claim that was undermined by her receiving her second high accomplishment award. All was going well until Veronica went to her family's home for a celebration of her cousin that was an extremely costly extravaganza. On her return, Veronica called to tell me she was having a "meltdown." She saw no point in continuing. She hated her husband. She hated herself. She hated me. She hated her job. She hated everything but her baby. After about 15 minutes, she paused in her harangue to catch her breath. I told her that she could rant at me as much as she needed. We had been here before. Her trip had set off her intense, painful envy. She was reexperiencing the world through her mother's envious devaluation of everything she had, her husband (Veronica's father), and her daughter unless she brought her continuous sources for bragging. I continued that as before the acute pain and terrible shame-filled drop in self-worth would fade, but the issue would not go away easily.

The next hour, Veronica repeated much of the same content but with less intensity and then reported a disturbing dream. She was somewhere when Pauline, a high school friend who was an animated loud athlete like Veronica, came in carrying a cobra. Everyone in the room was startled and frightened. Then, Veronica went to sit at a table and found herself next to Sue. She had always hated Sue—so quiet, so proper—but she had to admit Sue also was bright and was now a successful professional with a good marriage. Our analysis of this two-part dream brought together the problems of envy/shame and of gender identity. Veronica's mother was intensely envious of her successful misogynist brother and his wealthy sons and resented that she was unable to gain power by propelling her husband into equal success or to gain esteem on her own. In the household of Veronica's childhood, envy helped to turn everyone, male and female, into a snake with its symbolic male and destructive attributes. The mother's envious dissatisfaction with her husband (repeated at times by Veronica with Anthony) contributed to the father's raging (not so as yet with Anthony). The mother's envy spurred much of her needling (Chinese water torture) complaints about Veronica's legs, clothes, and weight and Anthony's presumed lack of ambition—giving her symbolic characteristics of a cobra's poisonous tongue. For Veronica, the search for power pressured her into incessant competition and accomplishment with an edge of simmering and sometimes eruptive rage and hatred. No snake, no power. No power only shame, failure and weakness. In the earlier dream of two tornados, the gender issue was clearer: Veronica, like her father, is a frightening rager. In the first part of the cobra dream, the snake/phallus, venomous tongue is grafted into a female athletic body—a male in a female to paraphrase Harris (2000). This aggressive phallic female startles and frightens people—the Veronica who can be very off-putting.

The second part of the dream moves the issue forward. Veronica reluctantly sits down next to Sue, who she ostensibly hates and disdains. Sue's representation throughout the analysis has been the conventional female (conventional having been Veronica's contemptuous designator for me and my wife). Sue is pretty but has no dazzle, is bright but is not a competitive star. Now in Veronica's associations, Sue, the feminine (without snake) female, had power and initiative if power and initiative mean a successful professional career, marriage, and being liked.

The calm that followed this understanding was brief before Veronica exploded again in discontent. She hated her life. Her project was taking up every minute at work. The minute she got home, she had to help with the baby. She had no time for the gym or to walk. She was back drinking to get calm and to go to sleep. Anthony helped, he was applying for a better job, and she was also. Talking to me was using up time she did not have. I thought to myself about the Chinese proverb, "Be careful of what you wish for." Veronica wanted a successful, intellectually challenging career; marriage; child; and home; now that she had them all, and I had helped to facilitate her getting them, she hated her life, and I could see why. Furthermore, I could see why I had not seen why before. Her successes had swallowed up her life; nothing was left that she felt was a choice just for herself, just for fun. To my embarrassment, I realized that despite all I had written about play, I had become so taken up with her overt goals that in a sense I also had been swallowed up. An analyst's similarity to a patient can be helpful in empathic understanding of the patient's goals from the patient's point of view, but it can also introduce blind spots. My own energetic approach, to do, to accomplish, mirrors Veronica so much that I became blind to her not balancing her life at all with all the sports, hobbies, and family fun that give my life the balance of choice.

I interrupted her I-hate-my-life harangue to tell Veronica that I could understand her discontent: Her life was devoid of anything she regarded as a time off from ambition, duty, and "just for her." I added that she had to remake her life pattern day by day, week by week, month by month. To my surprise, Veronica instantly agreed and began to consider specific just-for-her changes she could institute. She added that in a moment of clarity 2 days ago she had the thought that there was nothing wrong with her life; the problem was her. Veronica rapidly acted on her resolution to balance her life, and she and Anthony began to formulate realistic plans for their future.

This is not the end of Veronica's treatment, but I believe she had progressed to where she could view herself (Benjamin 1988) as "I, a woman; I a genderless subject; and I, like-a-man."

COMMENTARY

Looking backward from Veronica, what can be conceptualized about intimacy with the gendered self? I chose Veronica's case example because I believe her experience coincides with and confirms Benjamin's (1988) thesis presented in chapter 3. Veronica's mother, we can speculate, had surrendered her subjectivity and tried to restore a sense of desire and wholeness through submission to her idealized husband. He in turn regarded it his male privilege and prerogative to dominate his wife and daughter. The failure of Veronica's mother to provide her with a model of a woman capable of existence as a center for her own desires and agency forced Veronica to seek a similar solution in submission to other idealized males inclined to abusive dominance.

Veronica's experience also illustrates the compelling effect of a basic attachment disturbance. Not only was her mother not a source of desire and agency as a woman, but also she was not a source of protection as a mother. Not only was her father not a source of desire that was respectful and sensitive to his partner's needs, but also he was a source of fear, fright, shaming, and seduction. Stated differently, Veronica's domination–submission pattern played out against an overwhelming background of unresolved trauma, disorganization, and dissociation. As I suggested, I believe eroticized sadomasochistic domination–submission patterns are not only the product of maternal deficit in subjectivity alone but also reflect the effect of insecure attachment and other intrafamily disturbances (chapter 2). With secure attachment to both parents, culturally determined domination–submission relatedness is apt to be different in texture. Likewise, traumatic disorientation and dissociation can result from master–slave orientation between any member of a caregiver group regardless of gender.

Feminist, relational, and attachment theories all accentuate the incontrovertible significance of an intersubjective perspective. To be intimate with him- or herself, a boy or girl must know him- or herself in a relationship role with same- and other-gender friends, lovers, and enemies. A gendered self requires awareness of sex distinction. The intrapsychic perspective of traditional psychoanalysis made anatomy its central feature, valorized the phallus as Benjamin (1988) stated, and failed to recognize the mapping of self in relatedness with others as a basic schema. But, as I indicated, bodily sensation is a factor in the inner world of self that influences relatedness just as relatedness influences perception of one's body. The distinction between the more graduated experiences of sensual vitalization and soothing and the consuming expeence of orgastic excitement and relaxation is often omitted in accounts of gender development. Finally, all the theories have tended to accentuate dyadic relationships until an oedipal period, whereas mothers and fathers and babies often interact in loving, hating, and rivalrous possessive struggles that mark domination–submission themes early in life. Alternatively, the optimal protective umbrella for gendered self-development requires not the success of two dyads but the interplay of the caregiver unit or family system (Fivaz-Depeursinge & Corboz-Warnevy, 1999).

For women like Veronica, intimacy with her gendered self was not an inner world of playful confidence and happy sensual illusion. Contact with men, actual or in fantasy, activated a nightmare sense of herself as a woman. She viewed herself as exploited by her mother to soothe her father and to live out her mother's social and romantic ambitions and fantasies. Her view of herself in respect to her father was as victim of his temper, arrogance, and seduction. A major power he and other men exerted was the power to withhold themselves from her—a main source of her desperate torment of "He must come!" For women and for men who, unlike Veronica, have secure attachments and no proneness to disorganization and dissociation, intimacy with the gendered self can feel like a becoming a participant in a mutual playful sensual and sexual engagement, free of debilitating domination–submission.

As we approached the end of her analysis, Veronica was pregnant with her second child, her second major project was coming to a successful conclusion, and Anthony was choosing between two higher paying positions. Veronica stated: "When I am at work and all involved, I think this is great; I could do it all the time. When I am at home with my son and Anthony and the dogs, I think this is great; I could do this all the time." I commented: "And now you can do both and enjoy it and feel good about your achievement." She added: "Now with the two babies, I have to figure out how to be home more and find a way to consult from home or work part time. I know what I want and what I'm capable of, and I'll find a way to balance it."

CHAPTER 5

Fathers and Daughters, Mothers and Daughters

FATHERS AND DAUGHTERS

Of all the potential intrafamily dyads, the psychoanalytic view of the dyad of father and daughter has changed most dramatically over the century of analytic history. The historical starting point is the Freudian view of the patriarchal family: Mother and daughter are enmeshed in a fusion (ideally of mutual bliss). Father is essentially absent in the early stages and enters the dynamic scene as a disrupter of the mother–daughter symbiotic union. Father supplies the sense of time, order, and rules and a link to the outside world otherwise absent in the restricted world of cradle, kitchen, and playpen. Then, in the oedipal period the traditional Freudian view gets murky. The father–daughter dyad may simply mirror the conflicted path of father and son or is determined by the daughter's penis envy. The daughter's development requires an acceptance of passivity. Her oedipal love activates a desire that the daughter never renounces in the absence of castration anxiety and results in a less-structured superego. The adult daughter seeks a man like her father and through him relates to the world outside the home; while in the home, she achieves agency as housekeeper and mother.

Several contemporary perspectives challenge this stereotype. One perspective is that gender no longer connotes the fixity implied in "anatomy is destiny," but rather is a soft assembly (Harris, 2000) and plays out in a variety of ways in any father–daughter pair (chapters 3 and 4). A second perspective is that clinically father–daughter pairings take so many different outcomes that loose predictability seems a more useful premise than replacing the traditional category with a "newer, better" version. A third perspective points toward the usefulness of a developmental view of family systems dynamics that includes the mother and siblings as contributors to the playing out of the father–daughter experience.

The relationship of Freud and Anna Freud has become iconic in the literature on father–daughter relationships. Cohler and Galatzer-Levy (2007) played off Freud's fascination with myth by noting first the analogy of Freud–Anna to Oedipus–Antigone and then noting how Freud selected one part of the trilogy and ignored the other two. Antigone is more than a loving daughter; she led her ill elderly father into exile and a hallowed grave at Colonus, as Anna was to do for her father at Hampstead. Also like Anna, Antigone chose loyalty to her family's honor over marriage. Freud's analysis of his daughter revealed Anna struggled with masturbatory fantasies of a child being beaten, the consequences of incestuous desires, guilt, and regression to anal sadistic imagery. The "daughter" whose adolescent sexual drives Freud recognized was Dora. For both Anna and Dora, Freud portrayed the father as simply the object of the daughter's desire; his part in it, the cocreation I consider as both inevitable and desirable today, was absent from Freud's theorizing and as far as is known from his recognition of his own role. He was both father and analyst to Anna and was cloaked in "objectivity and neutrality." His need for her, as with Oedipus at Colonus, and its influence on her choices, especially sexual, remained outside the analytic canon of the father–daughter relationship. For her part, Anna combined ostensible absolute protective loyalty to her father's theories while contributing ideas that tilted the theory away from id and toward ego, and she broadened the conception of lines of development. Cohler and Galatzer-Levy concluded:

> The development of female sexuality had to forever remain unknown to Freud and his daughter because to recognize them, to assert female desire, would have meant to disrupt the bond between Anna and Freud. Father and daughter colluded to maintain a mystery so they might repeat the drama of Oedipus and Antigone. ... Both fathers accepted the care they received at the price of their daughters' full development, leaving the daughters ... forever ungratified sexually and forever tied to their fathers rather than forming families of their own.

Cohler and Galatzer-Levy suggested that Freud and Anna's denial of ordinary female sexuality "distorted the psychoanalytic vision of women's sexuality for decades."

Young-Bruehl (2007) regarded the Freud–Anna story from the perspective of a famous father and his youngest daughter. Young-Bruehl picks up on Freud's proposal of three inevitable relations that a man has with a woman: the woman who bears him, the woman who is mate, and the Mother Earth who receives him in death. Young-Bruehl stated that Anna proved herself to be Mother Earth, staying with her father to his death and "winning her struggle in the group of her siblings to be not number six but number one; and no longer disappointing to her father because she was not born a boy." I add that she also obliterated her mother, Martha, as a figure of consequence. So, taking up questions raised in chapter 2, we can ask, Was Anna an oedipal winner or loser, or was Freud an oedipal winner or loser? Freud won a lot—a devoted and brilliant follower, an intellectual heir (what he wanted from Jung), and a loving empathic caretaker. We could say he lost the pleasure of her marriage (which he at one time advised) and having her children to add to his pride in grandchildren. Anna won the contest with siblings and mother for her father's attention as daughter (and also analyst), the enormous pride of existence as his intellectual adherent, and the admiration both reflected from him and earned on her own.

According to Cohler and Galatzer-Levy (2007), she lost her opportunity for "full development," leaving her "forever ungratified sexually and tied to her father unable to form a family of her own." But, as Young-Bruehl reminded us (2007), Anna Freud's ties to her father did not prevent her from forming a loving secure attachment to Dorothy Burlingham, whether this attachment was sensual, sexual, or neither. Full development, like many other analytic mythic idealizations, is, I believe, difficult to define in an age in which a multiplicity of perspectives and subjectivity of view has replaced the hoped-for certainties of the age of reason that Freud inherited. However, perspectives aside, a troubled person's subjectivity does define pathological outcomes, and Young-Bruehl provided case vignettes of different disturbances of four youngest daughters: remaining daddy's little girl; defensively following in father's footsteps and martyr to his hopes for her; a mix of little girl and son without an ability to be intimate with anyone; and a housewife terrified of becoming anything else and miserable with envy of those who can be accomplished "in the world."

Not only is the patriarchal family no longer the expected standard of ordinary life and the average household no longer multigenerational, also we now find fathers who provide early bodily care of their daughters and who themselves experience the necessary symbiotic merger fantasies. Balsam (2007) described three young fathers whose successful care of their daughters indicated "mother love." As Balsam stated, "Maternal function cannot be attributed to inherent female biology but to psychodynamics." I regard a biologic mother caring for her newborn as having two advantages: She is hormonally primed, especially by ocytocin, for immediate attachment, and her baby is familiar with and comforted by her heartbeat as soon after birth as skin-to-skin contact is made. The playing field is somewhat leveled by the comparable existence in both mothers and fathers of procedural memory of their own infant care—a fundamental priming ready to be activated unless aggressively suppressed in males by the shaming of a particular culture. Finally, just as humans can be successfully fed by breast or bottle, human development is not narrowly instinctual but flexible with many fail-safe alternatives. Sometimes, I believe, our continuous professional encounter with psychopathology creates a bias against an appreciation of human creative adaptability. Balsam's report of the three primary caregivers produced a valuable balanced perspective. She pointed out two ways in which primary caregiver fathers differ from mothers: They bathe, diaper, and feed with a more vigorous, exciting quality (an observation Brazelton made years ago). When sexually aroused by their daughters, their erect penis is more apparent and potentially more guilt and shame inducing than a woman's less-notable signs of arousal. At the same time, Balsam describes how the fathers in her study were able to experience and contain sexual fantasies and arousal in their contact with their daughters' nubile bodies, thereby establishing rather than suppressing a sensual and erotic element in their relationship.

A study by Kiefer (2007) focused on the relationship between an older father and his daughter. She suggested that an optimal experience for a daughter with her father includes the development of her capacity for "an intimacy with otherness." Her development, in turn, creates for the father a new opportunity in midlife to further expand his own intimacy with otherness. Kiefer cited Aktar's (2005) description of the impact of a daughter on her father: By being more delicate and gentle in his handling of the daughter, he "gives up the satisfaction of his assertive-aggressive impulses; by keeping greater distance from the daughter's naked body he renounces voyeuristic impulses (an eye-vulva dialogue); he increases his cross gender knowledge and empathy; teaching his daughter skills, he becomes humbler in his masculine narcissism"; having to renounce sexual gratification while retaining a modicum of erotic resonance, he increases the "incest barrier" in his mind. My take on Aktar's prescription for optimal paternal influence is that, like most idealized modes of relating, it is probably rare and that might be just as well. Would it result in enough tension between daughter and father for the daughter to assertively set her boundary where she feels most comfortable? Would the daughter experience enough edginess in her erotic imagination of a partner who excites her to select an "otherness" of her personal choosing?

Kiefer (2007) noted that a father's romanticized trend to idealize his daughter may seduce her into a frustrated need to identify with and seek recognition from her knight in shining armor. Kiefer tracked the unhappy fate of the favorite daughter whose father requires her adoration or his self-worth. Because his love is contingent on a twinship merger with him, her autonomy is sacrificed. If she demands recognition as an independent person, then the father may react with astonishment and outrage. The daughter's traumatic disillusion may lead her in adulthood to avoid romantic entanglement or gravitate unconsciously to men with whom she will reenact the trauma.

Following Benjamin (1988), Kiefer (2007) described the "recognition" by father and daughter of the individuality of the other as a "mature selfobject function in which two subjectivities can idealize and mirror one another, while still retaining the notion of a selfobject bond in which there is a fundamental, non-pathological dependence." In my view, a nonpathological, dependent bond between father and daughter is sustainable and will include shared sensual exchanges, but for each to go about fulfilling personal sexual desires with someone else, a degree of subversion of the bond and the tension that results is necessary.

For a long time, conventional analytic "wisdom" stated that adolescent females should be treated by female therapists. Sometimes, this prescription extended to adult women with problems with sexual acting out. To discuss the pros and cons of this issue, Altman (2007) turned to his personal experience as the father of daughters and, with the encouragement of his wife, reconsidered the traditional constraint. In so doing, he recognized his strong maternal inclination exercised in shared caregiving with his wife. Further, as a pair, they reversed the usual gender–trait enactment; she was more apt to engage in rough-and-tumble play and he to downregulate the stimulation level. From each parent, the Altman daughters selected different traits and interests with which to identify and develop. Although his experiences as therapist led him to conclude his being male was generally not a defining feature, he became more aware, especially with some patients who lost their mothers in infancy, that his being a man did matter. He clarified that being a man is both a "brute fact" and the characteristic way in which he has come "to play being a man."

How a male analyst plays being a man is, I believe, a complex matter, touching on both his personal and his professional life. Obviously, how he deals with his sensual and sexual desires in his personal life, especially his latent frustrations, poses a challenge. How much or little satisfaction an analyst gains from his clinical experience is, I feel strongly, an underappreciated determinate of analysts seeking excitement in eroticized enactments. But, problems aside, males and females, analysts and patients, radiate to others' degrees of physical attractiveness—of being a stimulus for sensual and sexual excitement. Consequently, the analyst's unfolding persona as the analysis proceeds interacts with the analysand's unfolding persona in ways that trigger a variety of gendered, cross-gendered, and nongendered experiences.

In considering whether adolescent females need female therapists, Altman (2007) noted that frequently fathers who previously had been close to their daughters withdraw from them as the sensual and sexual tensions of puberty unfold. He concluded that although therapists cannot ignore dangers in any pairings with male and female adolescents, whether heterosexual or homosexual, "perhaps we need not be as anxious as we are."

Although sexual attraction is a given in psychotherapy with adolescents, it must be considered in all therapies. Traditionally, "it was the patient who desired and the analyst who contained," we now recognize that both parties can and will desire and contain. But, what about when sexual containment is lost? Altman (2007) suggested that a male therapist's fantasies of having a special reparative power in relation to a female patient camouflage his denial of his narcissistic neediness and exploitativeness. A male therapist locked in denial of his vulnerability may be under strong internal pressure to free himself of self-imposed controls by surrendering to a seductive woman. The seductive woman patient herself may be under pressure to use her wiles to overcome her feelings of powerlessness. Altman (2007) asserted that the development of postoedipal sexuality depends on the parent's capacity to let the child move away from the parent romantically and sexually, without shutting down an erotic level of the parent–child relationship. The narcissistic blow to the father of the loss of his daughter to the new oedipal victor of her age-appropriate choice is symbolized in Altman's ironic reference to becoming a "doddering father." Along with considering the erotic gains and losses for cross-gender patient–therapist pairings, Altman took up the advantage of same-sex pairings for the consolidation of identity. When an adolescent girl has had a serious disruption in her relationships with her mother, she may need a woman therapist to identify with while disidentifying with the depressed or traumatized mother. However, in the transference–countertransference interplay, a male analyst can enact and interpret both holding on to a female patient as did her mother and serve as a model of independence like her father.

As the father of three daughters, father-in-law to a daughter-in-law, and grandfather to six granddaughters, I find great compatibility with Altman's (2007) view of his role as analyst/therapist to female patients. As Altman implied, each male analyst comes to his task more or less prepared to accept the gender "assignment" called for by the needs of a particular patient. My early experience with an affectionate grandfather, a successful businessman who loved to cook special dishes learned from his mother and who loved to be with me, helped provide me with a background that made caregiving completely compatible with my notion of masculinity. My relationship with my grandfather was typified in adolescence when I gave parties in the townhouse in which I grew up. Coming home at 2 or 3 in the morning after taking my date home, as soon as I opened the door, I would hear my grandfather quietly coming down the stairs, saying: "Joe, I'll help you clean up so your mother won't be angry in the morning." Standing over the sink, washing and drying the glasses and dishes, he would ask who my date was, obviously sharing in my male adolescent quests, as we played out untraditional roles in the kitchen. For me, baby and child care—feeding, diapering, bathing, putting to sleep, fondling, rocking, cajoling, and correcting—came without threat to my sense of being male.

However, as my daughters grew and in encounters with my clinical "daughters," some tension and anxiety inevitably hovered over the explicit or implicit emergence of sexuality. During my residency training, a young woman who had been sexually abused by her brother and toward whom I had adoption fantasies asked me if she was sexually arousing me. I looked surprised and inquired what led her to ask. She pointed out that I was circling an ashtray with my finger. This provided a wake-up call to me to recognize my sexual responses despite shame or guilt. Eventually, with more training and experience, I came to recognize that without some arousal of desire on my part (or any analyst's part), a daughter in treatment is unlikely to be able to activate or form an experience of being desired and desirable. How I manage and employ beneficially my imaginary "love affairs" with my patient daughters is driven by the serendipity of each clinical situation. Harris (2007) described the requirement for the father both to delight in his daughter's emerging sexuality and maturity and to ruefully but steadily renounce his claim on her to continue to center her desire and admiration on him. He must both mourn and rejoice when "she moves to freedom and otherness in her self and in her loves."

A major contribution of Harris (2007) lies in what she calls a two-way street for desires, identifications, and oedipal engagements between fathers and daughters. Each must become a subject-object for the desire of the other, a desire constrained in actuality, freer in imagination. The daughter must be free to identify selectively with her father—sometimes in gendered aspects, sometimes in nongendered choices. The path of a daughter's identification with her father is well recognized in analytic theory, but Harris suggested and I strongly agree that optimally their link requires the father to open himself to a feminine identification to be able to experience and help his daughter to establish her full subjectivity. Harris's clinical contributions include case reports of fathers who are dangerous or lost and melancholy. Harris documented the importance of thinking of fathers and daughters as softly assembled systems within systems. Her narrative scenarios reveal the importance of paying attention to clinical individuality and recognizing the many ways in which gender may or may not be a salient feature of the character of any daughter and father at different moments of their lives.

Echoing Harris (2007) on systems within systems, I believe that consideration of the triangular nature of the family system adds to the exploration of father–daughter linkage. The dynamic effect of the mother in the play out of father–daughter relationship I believe has been understated. In the ordinary family constellation, a daughter's view of her father exists side by side with her view of her mother's view of him, sometimes in agreement or, at times, in violent disagreement. Babies as early as 3 months work to share their attention and affects with their parents (Fivaz-Depeursinge & Corboz-Warnevy, 1999). When engaged with either parent spontaneously, infants look to the other parent to bring him or her into the engagement. It is as if the infant is saying, I'm having fun with her or him, won't you join in; or, isn't it strange what he's doing, mother what do you think? Some families cooperate in having comfortable ways of sharing each other's attention and involving each other playfully. Some families are stressed but work tactfully and purposefully to overcome the problem. In other families, even with a baby at 3 months, one parent can be observed to capture and hold the attention of the baby—to form a collusive alliance that overrides the baby's natural inclination to include both parents. Other families operate so chaotically than at any moment the needs and desires of any member can be obliterated by the disorganization. When we recognize that at 10 months an infant reads his or her mother's facial expression to gauge if the presence of another person is to be viewed as welcome or dangerous, we can appreciate the significance of the father as seen through the eyes of the mother. A daughter may reject or accept her mother's view of the father, but she will inevitably be influenced by it. The opposite is especially true in that the father's appraisal of the mother influences the daughter's view of her own gender and herself.

Veronica's experience of her father had all the variance of their respective complex characters. As a child, she had been pulverized by his ferocious temper. Consciously made anxious (as he himself was) and behaviorally avoidant of a temper outburst, she unconsciously identified with father, with the "tornado" leaving her paralyzed in effective assertion until well into her analysis. She ridiculed him for his foolish displays of fear and rage while open to his seductive charm. He relied on her to get him out of his sulks, and she relied on him for the same. She admired his success in business and the wealth he provided and clearly wanted to follow his path to achievement outside the home rather than her mother's path as social matron. She chose her own professional path rather than his or her mother's brother and his sons. She felt sympathy for him as the victim of frequent invidious comparisons by her mother of his level of success in comparison with her mother's more successful brother. In analysis, a great deal of understanding was required before she could see any value in a man other than the power to hurt and withhold (as her father exhibited) or the power to be rich, have renown, and be arrogant, as her mother admired in mother's brother.

MOTHERS AND DAUGHTERS

Psychoanalysts of all theoretical positions agree that the oedipal myth about a male child provides an unsatisfactory model for either female development or the relationship between mothers and daughters. The Persephone myth suggested by Kulish and Holtzman (1998) gives primacy to a mother's relationship to her daughter in a triangular situation with a man. However, as I suggested in chapter 2, the myth of male abduction and mother's distress at her loss strikes me as portraying a daughter more as an object of possession than a subject of mutual sensual or passionate sexual love. The narrative of the myth plays out as a custody battle over a passive child decided by the court of gods, who award each contesting parent alternating custody. Persephone is given no choice by either contesting party. Her only agency or expression of desire resides in her eating the pomegranate seed, giving her a grown-up casting as a pregnant woman. The myth gives to Persephone the affirmation of being desired, but awards her with the barest modicum of being a source of desire (Benjamin, 1988), sexual or otherwise, or of being a center of initiative in Kohut's (1971) terms.

Notman (2006) suggested another myth: Mozart's *Magic Flute* presentation of the mother, the Queen of the Night; the father, Sarastro; the daughter, Pamina; and the lover, rescuer, Prince Tamino. Notman pointed to the puzzling transformation of the portrayal of the characters; in Act 1 the queen mother, distraught at the abduction of her daughter presumably by Sarastro, a wicked sorcerer (but actually by Sarastro's love-struck assistant). Then, in Act 2, Sarastro is presented as innocent of the abduction and a wise powerful protector; the queen appears as a wicked witch. Although Mozart's intention was to depict humankind's successful passage through ordeals to reach wisdom, a glorification of the Masonic movement, Notman interpreted the story as a developmental tale for Pamina in her relationship with her mother. Pamina and the audience realize that Sarastro's presumed villainy is a construct of her possessive mother. Notman postulated that the queen mother is transformed and demonized so that Pamina, with the support of a man, can leave her. The abduction saves the daughter "from owning the aggression and sexuality that the separation involved" (p. 138). "Her aggression is projected onto her mother the wicked one" (p. 138). In the end, she develops her own voice and expresses her desire in her choice of the prince—a mutual expression of romantic love. Pamina returns the Magic Flute to the prince, now her lover, and tells him that her father made it, an act Notman believed symbolizes the father's blessing.

Although the Magic Flute myth portrays the passivity of the daughter in the beginning (a possession to be abducted and fought over), Mozart's story gives her a voice (and beautiful arias to sing), choice, and desire in the end. But, the narrative retains the either–or problem of libido theory: Mother is good and father is wicked, so give up desire for him and stay with her; no, mother is wicked and father is good, so give up attachment to her and go with him. To desire the man, the mother–daughter link must be broken aggressively and dissolved. Mozart's version as interpreted by Notman presents the daughter with a situation in which she can follow her desire for her father and her prince, but at the cost of devaluing and demonizing her mother. Thus, both the Persephone myth and the Magic Flute narrative place the daughter in an either–or dilemma with which psychoanalysts fully concurred until recently.

For a long time in the development of psychoanalysis, *libido* was conceived of as a finite source of energy. Based on the libido theory, a girl had to take three developmental steps to achieve heterosexuality. She had to relinquish clitoral masturbation for the libidinal cathexis to flow to her vagina. She had to relinquish any male aggressive tendencies or identifications so the libido would cathect a female, more passive presentation. She had to relinquish her mother, that is, her original love object, for her libido to cathect her father as a heterosexual love object. Now, when affection and enjoyment are no longer regarded as a closed system or a zero-sum game, a girl can enjoy the sensations of her clitoris and her vagina, have male tendencies and identifications and still feel wonderfully feminine, and can feel love, affection, and devotion to both her mother and father. Addition is the mode of the developmental game, not relinquishment. But, in the open system mix and match, some sensations, some traits and identifications, and some forms of love, affection, and devotion will be more or less dominant at different ages and in different contexts. So, if the mother is never given up as a love object to turn also to father sensually and sexually, if, according to Kulish (2006), "a daughter's a daughter the rest of her life" (p. 7), then what are the dominant features of their relationship?

A daughter may experience her mother as reliable caregiver or unavailable when she needs her; as model to be like or model to be the opposite of; as angel or witch; as encourager or competitor; as sensitive or intrusive; as best friend or rival to best friend; as mentor or critic; as competent or ineffective; as wooer or rejecter; as generous or selfish; as sponsor to a full life or possessive; as compassionate or harsh; as beautiful or too fat, too thin, too made up, too plain; as attractively sensual or too sexy, too sexless; as the wonderful grandmother to her children or the demander of total preoccupation to mother's welfare. A mother may experience her daughter as gentle and responsive or pushy and difficult; as pretty and loveable or too fat, too thin, too squirmy; as devoted or selfish; as agreeable or too self-willed; as able to stand up for herself or too easily pushed around; as very like her mother and that is good or that is bad; as very like her father and that is good or that is bad; as independent and that is good or that is bad; as dependent and that is good or that is bad; as attractive to males and that is good or that is bad, whorish, and dangerous; as a rival to enjoy competing with or to be crushed; as a dependable helper and caregiver or too unavailable; as a person whose successes are a source of pride or are the key to a vicarious repair of all the mother's disappointments; as the provider of grandchildren to be adored or to have no obligation to husband or children that would interfere with her availability to provide care for her mother during illness or old age.

Veronica's (chapter 4) relationship with her mother provides an example of the nonlinear complexity of a mother–daughter dyadic experience. From our analytic reconstruction, I picture Veronica's mother as a devoted, probably moderately overanxious, caregiver. I see her as affectionate both in response to her healthy pretty baby and with strong needs to have affection returned to bolster her sense of loveability. She was inclined to be all over Veronica, dressing her as a Barbie doll. Her hovering contributed to the contrast of abandonment experience for Veronica when her mother's diabetic crises resulted in unexpected, unpredictable "absences." Veronica experienced her mother's hyperattentive preoccupation as living off her vicariously by bragging about her successes in school and in athletics. But, much success was not enough. Veronica, although popular, was not popular enough. Especially problematic for her mother was that Veronica's pretty face and athletic body were hampered, even in danger of ruin, by her stocky (fat in her mother's mind) legs. Veronica fought off her mother's critique as best she could, but she could not avoid painful self-consciousness about her legs, and in her analysis we engaged in much discussion about this painful blot on her self-image. Veronica was assigned by her mother to be a buffer between her mother's and father's temper, keeping him happy with her smile. More broadly, Veronica was to provide reparative solutions to all the arenas in which her mother's envy was stirred. A serious lack Veronica felt from her mother and to a lesser extent from her father was space—space to be free of the emotional overload of their requirements.

She paid dearly to gain the experience of a freer state through addiction to smoking, alcohol, and dissociation.

I conclude with two vignettes: One indicates the deep unconscious closeness of a mother and daughter; the second indicates the complexity of mother–daughter and father–daughter gendered assembly.

Marie was approaching the completion of a rather lengthy analysis. Intercourse with her husband was no longer avoided by her and was no longer experienced as primarily painful. The tragic ending of her love affair with her overtly seductive father's death and probable suicide had been mourned with much sadness. Marie described a dream of a king and queen who were both lovers and contesters. We saw the dream as an indication of the current state of her sexual life with her husband, a vast improvement over their prior sexual incompatibility. Then, Marie began to describe an aesthetic experience of photographing a magnolia bud. As I listened in a relaxed state, I was aware of the soft musical tone of her voice (quite unusual, I realized later). I drifted into a reverie in which I imagined Marie as a little girl gently fondling her clitoris. What leaped out at me from my reverie was the word *gentle*—a new experiential entry onto the stage of our analytic exchanges. This sensual element was what was missing in the pair's lovemaking and in Marie's life in general, establishing gentleness as a final theme in our analytic work.

A year and a half before the king and queen dream and the magnolia bud interpretation about gentleness, Marie, on my recommendation had sought analysis for her 9-year-old daughter, who was experiencing difficulties in her peer relationships and was frequently oppositional with Marie. Two years after Marie completed her analysis, in a chance conversation with the analyst treating her daughter, he told me the character of the analysis had undergone a dramatic shift for the better. As we talked further and checked on the timing of the shift, both of us believed the change in Marie, her openness to gentleness—to her own body, to her sexual relations with her husband, and to her dealings with her daughter's body and ways of their being together—played out as a powerful unconscious reparative form of implicit communication in the mother–daughter dyad.

Tandy began treatment in an extremely upset state. Her hair was falling out, her eczema was worse, and she was afraid she might be going crazy. Her mother had had a series of psychotic depressions, hospitalizations, and electric shock treatments. Each time Tandy called home and heard a worried tone in her mother's voice, Tandy became anxious and depressed herself. Her father looked after her mother, driving her to the doctor and getting her medicine. His mild-mannered reassurances to Tandy about her mother's condition did little to relieve Tandy.

Tandy was a moderately successful professional woman in her mid-30s. She was thin and attractive with a pleasant mild manner. Before her professional training, she had been a schoolteacher. She had taken each step in her life as if it were a big leap she might not be able to make. In her current work situation, she was harassed by male seniors, who were put off by her timid manner and careful obsessional approach when they wanted more risk taking. In her 20s, she had consulted a therapist, who had helped her to gain the confidence to go to a professional graduate school. Recently, she had been seeking understanding and solace from her married younger sister, who lived on the West Coast. Her sister had become impatient and frustrated, leaving Tandy to feel she could turn to no one.

With regular therapy sessions and the adjunctive help of medication, Tandy's original symptoms abated, and Tandy began long treatment with me. With many bumps in the road, Tandy changed firms a number of times, winding up in a prestigious position, in which she is highly regarded but still vulnerable to bullying by arrogant men and sometimes women as well. She is married and gets along well enough with her step-children, with whom she is more teacher and advisor than "mother."

Over time, my understanding of Tandy's core relationship to her mother and father changed dramatically. Originally, I regarded Tandy as having a preoccupied attachment to her mother. I viewed their mutual attachment as so entwined that Tandy absorbed into her being her mother's anguish and depression—a pathological codependent accommodation. I thought her sister had an avoidant attachment that freed her to live outside an overt mother–daughter entanglement. Gradually, I learned that in early childhood Tandy's sister had been enclosed with their mother in a symbiotic state, and Tandy had used school to pull away from her mother. Tandy sided with her father on many value areas, especially their opposition to aspects of religious fundamentalism and guilt that contributed to the mother's illness. In this family, the father was the sponsor of the girls' life outside the home; the mother wished for both daughters to remain close to her, sending not so subtle signals to Tandy that she regarded Tandy's marriage as a betrayal. I began to see that Tandy's preoccupation with her mother's upset states was to an extent an identification with her mother based on the intrusive effect of the mother's disruptive affect, and the preoccupation was to a greater extent an identification with her father as a devoted (probably guilty) caretaker. Her father was both the sponsor model for Tandy to develop a work life replete with travel and hobbies and the model for her anxious, obsessional fear of risk taking. Throughout Tandy's childhood, her father worked as a low-level professional for a large midwestern company. He felt constantly underappreciated for what he did and harassed unfairly by superiors. Between the father's constant fear of losing his position and the mother's recurrent depressions, the family lived as if under siege. Looked at in this way, Tandy's timidity, vulnerability, and insecurity could be regarded as Tandy's identification with the family system rather than a specific individual. Tandy's sister's avoidant strategy would possibly be a flight from the whole family system.

Focusing on Tandy's gender identity provides a look at more particular sources of femininity and masculinity. Tandy had many qualities of "I, a woman." She dressed stylishly: She and her mother loved to go shopping. She had an infectious giggle-laugh: She and her mother liked to joke and gossip with each other. She had several romantic attachments and at least one lust-filled affair with a culturally unlikely man. On the "I-like-a man" side, she was professionally ambitious—like her father. Along with her timidity, she exhibited a quiet courage with which she faced adversity—also like her father.

My concluding point is this: Whether considering Veronica, Marie, Tandy, or any of the patients to whom I refer, a daughter's gendered self is the outcome of a complex nonlinear process of multiple experiences and the particular, often-unpredictable responses the individual makes to those exposures to parents, family, and many others she meets along the way. Psychoanalysis permits both patient and analyst to appreciate the complexity of anyone's gender assembly and to achieve a healthy intimacy with the potential multiplicity experience offers.

CHAPTER 6

Middle Childhood and Adolescence

MIDDLE CHILDHOOD

I have chosen the term *middle childhood* to emphasize the active developments that occur during this period rather than the absence of activity implied in the more conventional term *latency*. Latency was an appropriate libido theory designator for sexuality during the period between the waning of the oedipal complex and the onset of puberty. During these years of elementary school into junior high, the intensity of libido as evidenced by pressure for sexual excitement was markedly diminished as compared with the period before and after; therefore, the libidinal energy was regarded as latent rather than active. Latency also referred to the recognition that the sexual fantasy and dream life during middle childhood was latent in the sense that it was always present and potentially emergent if stimulated. But, latent points more to absence than presence, and observation of children in these middle years clearly indicates the presence of important manifestations of the sensual–sexual motivational system. I discuss the significance during middle childhood of working out gender themes and the importance of friendships.

Middle childhood is a period of life during which the exploratory–assertive motivational system frequently dominates the child's consciousness—in school, on the playground, in pursuit of hobbies, and in an expanding view of the world outside the narrower confines of the family. From the standpoint of the sensual–sexual motivational system, middle childhood offers the opportunity to explore gender roles freed of pressure to seek and link with a romantic partner. However, much of what comes after in the partnering phase of adolescence is prefaced and prepared for in middle childhood friendships, especially "best friends." Sroufe, Egeland, and Carlson (2005) stated:

> Maintaining boundaries between genders is a normative occurrence
> in middle childhood. Only 6% of observed interactions were with

children solely of the opposite gender in our camps. In some cultures adults enforce separation between genders in preadolescence. ... But in Western industrialized countries, children must maintain these boundaries themselves. When children interacted with members of the other gender in our (camp) study, they did so with the "protection" of same-gender partners or had some other form of "cover" (a counselor made them do it, it was inadvertent, etc.), or they disavowed the contact through name-calling. ... Moreover, boundary violations were followed by sanctions (teasing, ridicule, and innuendo) by members of the child's own gender. (p. 153)

Sroufe et al. (2005) viewed the purpose of boundary maintenance as providing children the opportunity to practice intimacy in a safe social context. I agree but believe that, in addition to practicing intimacy, boundary maintenance and freedom from pressure to seek a sexual partner allow children to work out and play out different aspects of gender— what complex mix of being a boy or girl he or she will assemble. Harris's (2000) studies of tomboys provide an excellent example of one solution to what complex manner of girl that a particular girl will sort out to be in middle childhood. "The tomboy's identity, a boy in a girl, a boy and a girl, a girl and more than a girl, a girl whose phallic activities may be dystonic or syntonic, these are all shifting self-states at play" (p. 228). Many different strategies can lead to a tomboy identity: the conviction that women are second-class citizens, weak or ill; that being male is the only site of excitement; that boyness is the only route to maternal (or paternal) care and affection; that being a tomboy will keep her brothers from abandoning her as playmates; that being a tomboy protects her from the danger of penetration and damage or from temptations toward premature promiscuity. In each instance, the strategy may reflect the acceptance or rejection of a parent's conscious or unconscious desire that has been explicitly or implicitly conveyed to the child. The impact of a father's and mother's fantasies and desires for him- or herself and for a daughter or son will impact the child differently if the parents are in accord with one another or oppositional.

Middle childhood boys struggle among themselves about manliness and courage in various structured and unstructured modes of rough-and-tumble organized sports and impromptu schoolyard challenges. A boy struggles to find his place in a shifting hierarchy between "bully and sissy." Can he feel masculine being the boy he is—good at this, not good at that, brave about this, scared of that? Can he comfortably incorporate into his soft assembly of gendered characteristics those that might be considered feminine: studiousness; cooking or hanging out in the kitchen; gentleness with his little sister; a liking of nature, flowers, his mother's perfume? And, while this is largely played out in a male-boundaried world, in his peripheral vision and fantasies, he is aware of girls and how one or another particular girl regards him (institutionalized on Valentine's Day).

Popularity is the basis of the social status of middle childhood girls, and popularity is based on attractiveness, charm, knowing the right things to say, knowing the right clothes to wear, and finding the right mix between brashness and shyness. How popular a girl is may carry not only her own desires but also all the wishes and disappointments of her mother, as illustrated by Veronica (chapter 4). In paradoxical contrast between the cultural concern about boys as too studious and unathletic and therefore unmanly "nerds," girls in the past had been warned against demonstrating how smart they were because boys would be frightened off: More brains meant a weaker phallus in the value system for boys of macho fathers, and more brains and being an athlete meant a girl had a stronger phallus in the phallocentric world of submissive mothers. A particular gendered problem girl's work out within the boundary of gender boundary separation is bodily display. Although boys commonly display their muscles and athletic prowess, the tension as an object of an erotized gaze is much greater for girls. Penetrating eyes are an anxious concern of middle childhood girls before physical sexual penetration is an issue. To show too much may be embarrassing; to want desperately to show is shameful; not to be noticed is disappointing and humiliating; to hide from notice is a painful abdication of desire.

Thus far, I have discussed the playing out in middle childhood of gendered aspects of self. When does sensuality and sexuality enter the picture? I believe we need to examine the great importance of friendships, especially best friends during this period. Sroufe et al. (2004) referred to the formation of close friendships as the hallmark of middle childhood. They reported that those children with secure attachment histories spent 39% of their time with a close friend, and those with anxious attachment histories spent 25% of their time with a close friend. The children with anxious histories often crowded others, standing too close, touching too much. Those with particular problems in maintaining self–other boundaries had histories of disorganized attachments and parent–child physical and sexual violation.

Sroufe et al. (2004) observed there were

> variations in how children balanced the complexity of interacting with same- and other-gender children, functioning in groups, and maintaining close friendships. Potentially, a friendship could be a boost

to group acceptance and participation, and being in groups could advance functioning in friendships through providing new opportunities and formats for balance. (p. 155)

If two friends with secure histories were chosen to be on competing teams, then they maintained eye and verbal contact. Alternatively, for children with anxious resistant histories, the stimulation of group participation could overwhelm their capacity to maintain contact with their friend. Pairing of two children with avoidant attachment histories was rare, with the partners preferably playing separated from others and avoiding group activities.

Looked at closely, we can observe the erotic elements evoked in the best friend experience of boys and girls in middle childhood. In locker rooms, stimulated by each other's naked bodies, boys will engage in towel fights, whooping and screaming in their sensual excitement. Both boys and girls in sleepovers will express their arousal by bouncing on beds and engaging in pillow fights. In other words, an erotized or sensual element is an inescapable aspect of close friendships. Particularly for girls (and to a less-demonstrable degree for boys), the shifting sands of best friend plays out all the themes of later romantic love. All of the elements of dyadic and triadic sensual relatedness unfold: the wooing; the coming together; the private and public pledges; the meaningful glances; the special language, jokes, and secrets; the spats; the rivalries; the temptations posed by a seductive other; the betrayals, abandonments, longings; and the lasting resentments on breaking up. Particularly in the older prepubertal children, longing for the company and companionship of the best friend often includes stirrings of erotic desire that may be frightening and defended against because of homoerotic implications. The object of sensual desire may be the best friend or an older teenager (e.g., camp counselor, teacher, coach).

Case Example:
Transition from Middle Childhood to Adolescence

Jane's mother, Mrs. B., called and said her 13-year-old daughter had confided in her that she was coming home from school, eating, and then throwing up. I arranged a time for mother and daughter to come in, but Jane appeared alone, explaining that she did not wish to burden her mother. Jane stuck me as a bright, sincere teenager, mature for her age, and I liked her immediately. She explained that her bulimia began shortly after her family moved to the United States from Europe. Her mother was an American from a well-known intellectual family. Her father, although from a working-class European family, had obtained an advanced degree and had come to the United

States to teach at a university. After two sessions, Jane called and said she could not continue. She regarded coming for therapy as disloyalty to her family, especially to her father, because the cost would strain their limited resources.

A week later, Mrs. B. called and said she had discussed the matter with her husband, and he withdrew his objections; Jane would continue. Jane and I easily formed a relationship of mutual trust as she presented a coherent picture of her history, family members, and her current life at school. She felt she was different from many of her peers in that she loved her parents. She did recognize that she was distressed that her mother did not provide her with a model of strength and self-worth. She got along okay with a few girls at school but did not believe she was popular and felt excluded from the in-groups. She had had two best friends in Europe, with whom she still corresponded. She also felt different in that she was a talented writer, having won competitive prizes. We tracked the ups and downs of her bulimic symptoms, relating this to the stresses of the moment. A frequent theme was her sympathy and concern for her father, who had suffered a loss in his family in Europe. A main focus of our work was on my encouraging her to delve more into the feelings triggered in her by the events she was relating, especially disappointment, anger, and criticism of her idealized parents and their overly protective restrictions in comparison to the unusual American freedom of teenagers.

In one session, Jane described a particularly severe episode of bulimia. As the session drew to an end, Jane began to cry and in an unusually distressed voice appealed to me directly: "What shall I do?" In a voice that I am certain conveyed my responsive distress, I spontaneously answered, "Feel!" As I sat a bit stunned by the unusual directness of this exchange, Jane got up mumbling, "Feel. I have to feel," and left. The next session, Jane reported she had confronted her mother about her anger at her mother for a specific instance of submissiveness, overaccommodation, and obsequiousness. And, she added proudly, she had not thrown up.

As Jane's suppressed emotions became more available during the hours, she began to experience a flood of sadness about her mother's plight as the least-esteemed member of a creative family. Jane feared that her closeness to her mother might keep Jane herself from developing her own potential. At the end of an hour just before a break, Jane was unusually upset. With tears still flowing down her face, she put her hand out to shake my hand. Jane had initiated our shaking hands as part of her European culture, and it became both a convention and an opportunity to exchange looks of mutual affection. On this occasion, her hand seemed to me to linger, although I cannot say I consciously thought it. In turn, without plan, my left hand rose to encompass her hand, and we stood for a minute of eye contact and exchanged emotion.

As these patterns were effectively explored, another voice entered. Jane, wearing very short shorts, began to cross and uncross her legs. She would flex her back, pushing her developing breasts forward. All the while, she was talking and listening to me as before with no apparent recognition of the "sexy body" dance she was performing. Her body seemed to be entering our conversation as an independent agent. From the standpoint of motivational systems, two needs were pressing for dominance: the defended-against aversive attachments we were discussing explicitly and a state of sensual–sexual arousal we were enacting implicitly. However, she consciously recognized only one of these motivational themes as integral to her immediate sense of self. I considered whether to address the emergent body message or wait. I felt certain that were I to call her attention to her wiggling around she would become painfully self-conscious, and that the embarrassment could adversely affect the budding emergence of her adolescent sensuality. Alternatively, I considered whether the embarrassment I was concerned about was hers or mine. Was I participating in an enacted disavowal of an oedipally based seduction of me? Was I overprotective, as were her parents? I chose to wait, and 2 weeks later Jane reported that something very unexpected had happened. A boy who had always ignored her sat beside her at lunch, and they were going to a movie together.

Over the next several years, with remarkable candor, Jane described to me the full unfolding of her sensual and sexual explorations. With considerable maturity, she pushed and pulled her parents into supporting her with appropriate structure and freedom. I was struck that especially at first she made choices based primarily on what she felt her body was telling her, with the relationship secondary. Gradually, her choices were made more frequently on the meaningfulness of the romantic attachment as she struggled through the usual mid- and late-adolescent "heartbreaks."

For the remainder of the school year when puberty "struck." Jane's dating was casual and relatively anxiety free, and her bulimic episodes were rare. She went to Europe for her summer break to stay with her former best friend. On her return, with a mixture of pride and slightly embarrassed hesitation, she described the events of the summer. Her hostess had moved from middle childhood into full-bloom adolescence as part of a group of males and females who all went together in a "pack" and paired off for sensual and sexual exploration. Jane paired off with one teenaged boy she really liked, and they engaged in pleasing petting. During a period when he was traveling with his family, Jane paired off with another boy—slightly older and more experienced—and had her first intercourse. I was struck that her mode of describing this event was businesslike and purposeful. Jane stated that she knew she would be doing it some-day, and this seemed a good opportunity. It was as if she was inter-ested in exploring the capacities of her body and confirming that she was a fully functional female. She and the young man had a pleasant relationship but little more. Her romantic feelings were directed to the absent teenager and resumed for a time on his return. I sensed that Jane intuitively felt that with the older boy their sexual encoun-ter would go off with no "strings," but with her more intimate part-ner the development of troubling emotional complications was more likely.

Once back in Washington, Jane began slowly to date, and we resumed exploring her emerging sexual desires and her shifting attachment to her family. As with many adolescents, Jane was wary of greater recognition and exploration of her deeper feelings—partly characterological, partially an adolescent's understandable need and wish for privacy. Facilitating our progress, Jane spontaneously introduced another mode of communication that helped us both. She had for a long time been a skilled writer. Now, her writing took on a more personal nature, and she brought many examples for me to read in her sessions. Part of Jane's talent was to use mythologi-cal events, literary references, and personal imagery as metaphoric expressions of her message. Often, I was unable to follow her poetic allusions. We began a pattern of my asking her to help me, which she did eagerly and, I was happy to note, without condescension or dis-dain for my ignorance. Somehow, these exchanges, so different from ordinary therapy discourses, opened a vein of deeper entry into how she was feeling about her body, her love of life, and me. For Jane and me, her writing and our discussions of them, rather than dreams, was the royal road. In Jane's words: "I begin to explore my life, a cautious web of nerves, a kaleidoscope of sunlit openings between us and the shore."

Jane indicated that she was desirous of maintaining an active sexual life when she connected with someone here. She also talked more about the alcohol and drug use among her peers. I began to experience increasing unease and struggled to resist a parental con-trolling attitude that expressed explicitly or implicitly would hamper the openness of our communication. Finally, I told Jane I was in full support of her expanding world of feelings, sensual relationships, and sexual desires, but some dangers did trouble me. She nodded agreement, and I told her that for my comfort I would ask her one question—about contraception. Pushing the issue aside with ease, she answered, "Oh, I talked to my mother, and she sent me to the gynecologist, and I'm all set." This exchange consolidated for me my view of Jane. Building on all our experience together, I concluded that Jane had what Kohut (1971) called a cohesive self with a center of initiative, what I call an inner gyroscope that would allow her to keep her balance despite the developmental stresses ahead of her and us. My confidence in Jane was put to the test in her senior year when, despite her parent's misgivings, she began to attend raves, large gatherings with strobe lights, rock music, and heavy drug use; these raves lasted late into the night. Jane's willingness to tell me about it in detail and her sensible judgment about what dangers were the ones to stay clear of reinforced my confidence. We were probably helped by my recognition of the many hazards I had negotiated my way through at a similar age.

I next became concerned that Jane was regarding sex solely as an enjoyable experience of lust with pleasant and suitable changing partners. Although this was temporally appropriate for a high school girl, the absence of any expressed desire for a deeper love relationship made me wonder if such a desire was absent or suppressed. Was Jane afraid of being hurt? Was she constrained by her wish not to be a submissive female like her mother and to have a more independent career life plan? Against this being the case was Jane's strong affection for her father and my sense of a cross-gender link to me confirmed in my feelings toward her. Then, in the middle of her senior year, Jane fell in love. Dwight was a junior, a half-year younger, bright and interesting, and the two became inseparable. Then, as the end of the school year approached, they began to drift apart. Jane experienced much heartache at the ending of her first real love affair but felt resigned as well. The core of her feeling of resignation was that she would be going off to college, and Dwight would not. She would be leaving him, her parents, and me. Again, I felt the two strands of Jane's motivational trends—to live in the moment with its ups and downs, its triumphs and defeats, and through it all to hold to a plan to be the capable, talented, loving adult woman she was on her way to become. In separating from Dwight, I believed Jane was saying to him and to me as well that she intended to clear the slate of her attachments to be open to whatever life in college was going to offer.

ADOLESCENCE

Tracking the sensual and sexual lives of adolescents in a period of changing sociocultural contexts is like following a fast-moving target. In the segment of the world where technology rules, adolescents have very early Internet access to knowledge about sexuality and are likely to delay full family commitment to much later (psychosocial moratorium; Erikson 1959/1980).

Parenthetically, in other parts of the world preteens and adolescents are often turned into soldiers and rapists. In the technological world, with the availability of total information about sexual practices, nudity, and chat room commentaries about the sex and social life of individuals all over the globe, young adolescents are beginning an active sexual life earlier. They are also modifying the prior sexual seduction sequence characterized in the United States by an analogy to baseball, with first base kissing, second base necking with fondling of breasts, third base fondling of genitals, and a home run or scoring as intercourse. In this sequence, oral sex was considered a postintercourse refinement or "advance," whereas today oral sex for adolescents may be practiced much earlier and as a substitute for intercourse. Pre-Internet, the main sources of sexual education were considerably more insular: neighborhood peers, movies, books, and less-available pornography. Post-Internet, a teen in Istanbul may tell all about his "love life" to a girl in Dallas, and each may provide visual information as well. And, when the Web page connections are more local, naïve adolescents expose themselves to predators and exploiters.

Aside from these risks, what are the clinical implications for adolescents of these sociocultural changes? Previously, adolescents figuratively and factually felt their way along in an exploration of crushes and openings to sensuality and sexuality, that is, learning by doing. Now, the Internet functions as a manual for seeing and instruction that is then put into operation. Sex between partners becomes less an expression of romantic love and more an exercise of learning a technique or "practicing sex as though it were an Olympic sport" (S. Doctors, personal communication, 2006). I experienced a comparable response to Jane when she described her sexual experience (experiment) in Europe in so businesslike a manner that I became concerned (unnecessarily) about her capacity for intimacy. A constant in the changing world of adolescent sexuality are the bodily transformations of puberty:

> At puberty the ovaries and testes begin to pour estrogen and testosterone into the bloodstream, spurring the development of the repro-

ductive system. Recent discoveries evidence that these sex hormones released by the adrenal glands are extremely active in the brain ... exerting a direct influence on serotonin and other neurochemical substances that regulate mood and excitability. (Ammaniti, Nicolais, & Speranza, 2007, p. 84)

Puberty is an emergent property of the biological substrate of the sensual–sexual motivational system. The pressure for change on the sense of self may be gradual and mild or sudden and intense, but the pressure is unyielding, and changes occur. From the vantage point of the distinction between socially affirmed expressions of sensuality and socially proscribed expressions of sexuality, recalibrations are forced on the developing boy and girl (self-regulation), parents (dyadic and triadic regulation), and on the larger social group (societal regulation). Some sensual activity, such as a boy kissing and hugging his father or his mother, may now be regarded as sexual. A previous case of dancing with and showing off before a parent may be replaced by self-consciousness on both sides. Opposite-sex partnering will be expected but often is the source of anxiety, and same-sex partnering is often a source of far-greater alarm and sometimes a source of intense attraction. Privacy on the adolescent's part may be recognized as needed but nonetheless can be a potential source of loss and concern for parents.

The hormonal "hit" on brain and body was apparent in Jane's sexy dance in my office and was out of her awareness but not out of the awareness of her male schoolmate. Thus began for Jane the switch from middle childhood's girls in one group and boys in another to adolescence's cross-gender dating. Popularity remains an issue but also switches to cross-gender issues and regrouping. The more glamorous popularity is that of the cheerleader and of the athlete (jock). Another is the popularity of the attractive, bright, talented good student girl and the talented good student boy (nerd). The best friend becomes fluid—maybe same or opposite gender or preferably both as confidant. A traditional analytic view held that adolescents subvert their attachment to their parents to individuate within peer groups. Counter to this view are the observations in attachment research and self-psychology that adolescents retain their basic ties to their parents despite their transgressive rebellious attitude toward present authority. Adolescent peer attachments and romantic love attachments do not replace parental attachments but add to these, as was clear with Jane. And, adolescents who establish peer and nonfamily adult confidants generally retain one or both parents as nonauthoritative confidants. Put another way, a secure base that remains available is never abandoned.

During the grand romanticism of the 19th century, the myth was formed of adolescence as a period of Sturm und Drang and was dramatized by Goethe in the suicidality of *The Sorrow of Young Werther*. Because pubertal sex hormones strongly affect the brain's emotional core, the limbic system, and trigger states of high excitement, adolescents develop an appetite for thrills, intense experiences, exaggeration, and excitement. Many adolescents become overwhelmed by one or more of the pitfalls of the period: risky sexual encounters, drug and alcohol abuse, and participation in antisocial group behavior. But, many do not, as revealed by Offer's (1980) careful studies. The legendary Sturm und Drang myth points accurately to the inclination for exciting enactments but leaves out the capacity for self-regulation and responsiveness to the regulatory input of parents or other mentors.

In Sroufe's studies (2005), having first intercourse at later ages was predicted by early positive care, peer competence, low behavior problems, and low family stress in elementary school. Alternately, the high sexual risk group had had poor childhood support, negative emotional family climate at age 13, gender boundary violations during middle childhood, poor parental monitoring during adolescence, and lack of motivation in school beginning as early as first grade. For boys, early age of first intercourse and promiscuous use of partners predicted getting a girl pregnant. For girls, gender boundary violations in middle childhood predicted more frequent unprotected sexual activity. Sroufe's attachment-focused studies connect earlier sexual abuse to some middle childhood gender boundary violations. However, the studies do not reveal which abused adolescents engaged in early sexual, substance, and other risky behavior.

Brain maturation may also influence risk taking. On one side is the maturation of intellectual capacities—the operational thinking noted by Piaget (1957)—that allows adolescents to tackle "school-based learning" more skillfully. This contributes to their sense of increased independence from parents, becoming more of an equal (I know as much or more than you), and a false sense of security in their judgment. On the other side is the slower rate of maturation of the area of the prefrontal cortex responsible for "executive planning and strategizing, setting priorities, organizing thoughts, suppressing impulses, weighing the consequences of one's actions" (Ammaniti et al., 2007, p. 84).

Prediction at any age is difficult and during adolescence even more so. Troubled, avoidantly attached adolescents may become isolated or pair off with others like them either in actuality or on the Internet. They may harbor destructive nonsexual or sensual fantasies that they may or may not act on. With their reduced sensitivity to the impact of sexual contact on themselves and a partner, intercourse psychically becomes either a "screw" or a rape. The more anxiously, resistantly attached adolescents tilt toward a more romanticized view of partnering. They often become preoccupied, endlessly talking about the ups and downs of each successful or failed contact. They may attempt to hide their embarrassment at failure by bragging to their friends about false claims of success. In daydreams or actuality, they may stalk their "love object" or invite domination by the other in hopes of ensuring attachment. Secure attachment offers the adolescent a background for navigating the stresses of adolescent sexual risks but provides no guarantee. Peer pressure, misjudgments about substances, and inexperience in gauging the intentions of others, especially psychopathic others, expose both securely and insecurely attached boys and girls to dangers in "partying," Internet dating, and high-speed driving.

Ammaniti et al. (2007) described an unusual opportunity to study a group of young adolescents engaging in group sex. Beginning with an episode of rape and blackmail, three girls aged 12 and 13 became compliant, secretive participants with a large group of 14- to 17-year-old adolescent boys in multiple episodes involving oral sex, masturbation, and intercourse. None of the participants formed a close or privileged relationship during the several months of their meetings. Barbara, well dressed and self-confident, gave global descriptions of family closeness and maternal support that were contradicted by numerous episodes in which her mother was absent, engrossed in her job, and unavailable during Barbara's illnesses. Barbara's self-portrayal was that she was compulsively self-reliant and autonomous. Shortly before the sexual episodes, Barbara's 18-year-old sister left home, and Barbara's mother had another daughter. Barbara's dismissing state of mind regarding attachment was mirrored by her mother's minimizing her daughter's and her own deep affective needs. The mother's own deprivation was compounded by her father's death when she was 6 and being sent to boarding school at the age of 12—all referred to with extreme detachment. Her wish for her daughter was simply "to be independent and to earn her own living."

Carol, aged 13, childlike, impetuous, and belittling to authority, was preoccupied with her mother's neglect of her and the favoritism shown to her brother. In contrast to these angry preoccupations, she was dismissing of her need for others, emphasizing her independence and autonomy, while holding a negative appraisal of herself and her body. She oscillated between infantile needs for reassurance about her negative self-image and pseudoindependent provocativeness. Carol's mother, who had been a parentified child to her mother, existed in a state of intense anxiety and preoccupation both about Carol and her own childhood attachment experiences. Surprise, confusion, disorientation, and disbelief were her response to Carol's actions despite cognitive awareness of Carol's jealousy of her brother.

Alicia, well dressed and looking older than 12, was an only child whose parents, especially her father, took great pride in her abilities and attractiveness. But, emotional responsiveness in the family centered on embraces and physical care to the body at the expense of more mature reflection. Unlike Barbara's avoidant attachment and Carol's unclassified (mixed avoidant and preoccupied) attachment, Alicia was classified as secure with some elements of preoccupation. She could talk coherently and openly about her childhood relational history. Alicia's mother, also classified as secure regarding attachment, nonetheless described a history of overinvolvement with her parents, in whose bed she slept until her marriage at 18. In the 2 years prior to the incident, Alicia's mother had traumatic losses of her brother and parents, leaving her unresolved for trauma. Ammaniti et al. (2007) suggested that the mother's absorption in mourning may have been a precipitating factor for Alicia.

What a psychological puzzle this was to unravel! Ammaniti et al. (2007) presented as their main explanatory approach the impact of the girls' attachment strategies and the transgenerational link to their mothers' attachment category. They added precipitation factors in two cases and conjecture about the impact of peer relations. Barbara and her mother were both avoidant regarding attachment and heavily invested in pseudoautonomy. Carol oscillated between dismissive and preoccupied strategies; her mother was intensely anxious and preoccupied. Alicia was secure regarding attachment, with some preoccupation; her mother, also secure regarding childhood attachment, was currently unresolved regarding three recent losses of family members. No explanatory pattern leaps out of the attachment classifications. As for precipitating events (Alicia's mother's mourning, Barbara's older sister having left, and Barbara's mother having another daughter), each case possibly diminished the young adolescent's sense of someone to care for and about her. Another precipitating event for each girl was making the transition from middle childhood, through puberty, into adolescence with a body that was saying how grown-up she was and a mind that had not yet matured to the operational level of full recognition of consequences. The authors gave weight in Alicia's case to a sudden and drastic need to seek attention from other figures. I believe this was true of all three girls and is to a lesser extent also true for all young teens.

But, what led these girls to the final common pathway of secret group orgies? For example, although Alicia's parents were sufficiently available for establishing a secure base, were they dangerous in overstimulating her physically while overinvesting in her attractiveness (her mother had slept with her parents until married). Were any of the girls attracted to activities that were transgressive of ethical and moral rules? Only Carol appeared rebellious. Were any attempting to repossess their body self from an enmeshing entanglement with one or both parents? This was possibly true for Alicia from her overinvested father. Were any of the girls enacting a deep, deep resentment of their parents? Possibly, Barbara was, with her simmering rage about her brother's entitled position.

Attachment research focuses on the relations of the child to a primary attachment figure, but the mother is also a source of identification in a girl's structuring of her gender identity. The mother's femininity is not an entity; it is a changing "communication" to be read by her daughter as the mother stands before a mirror, as the daughter registers how her father and other men look at her mother. And, a daughter compares the looks her father gives her mother with the looks he gives her or her friends and what joy, disgust, or neediness is conveyed. Through look and touch, excessive sexualized physical intimacy may be intergenerationally transmitted. This powerful transmission may remain largely unrepresented symbolically, with the resulting physical excitation becoming in some instances a salient aspect of the parent–child relationship. The story of intergenerational transmission of excessive sexualized physical intimacy with mother, father, grandparent, or sibling is difficult to access by attachment or family research or by psychoanalytic-based single-case approach alone. Especially important in understanding sensuality and sexuality in adolescents are the secrets of peer relations: whether a we world of reexploring morals and ethics and broadening one's range of intimacy or a we world of silence, conspiracy, misleading mutual loyalty, and transgressive destructiveness or raw sexuality without attachment as with Barbara, Carol, Alicia, and the large group of 14- to 17-year-old boys.

At a particular moment or series of moments, something crystallized experientially for each of the three girls (and their male counterparts) that led to an addictive surrender to the immediacy of a powerful conscious or unconscious desire. Was it for bodily excitement with or without pain? Was it for a fantasy of being a movie star, a queen, a whore? Was it to "stick it to her parents" for one empathic failure or another? Was it to do with her body what she damn well pleased? Was it to do with the boy's body what she or he wanted? Was it to be a member of a transgressive cult of superior or inferior beings? Was it for any or all other imaginings, fantasies, and beliefs? Did the girls become more impaired in forming a later romantic attachment than would be expected from Barbara's avoidant pattern, Carol's oscillating preoccupation and avoidant pattern, and Alicia's secure pattern? Did Alicia's secure attachment to a securely attached mother provide her with a greater capacity for self-righting, for resilience? But, most of all, what was in each family's life that was not conducive to a respectful approach to the mind and body and the feelings and intentions of each member? Does an attention to attachment, with its dyadic implications, tilt inquiry away from triadic intrafamily considerations and especially the role of fathers in the life of daughters (chapter 4)?

During adolescence, the balance between sensuality and sexuality established in childhood tilts toward sexual desire and cross-gender partnering (usually, but of course not exclusively). The tilt toward accentuated sexual desire ushers in the subversive and transgressive pressures that I believe are the hallmarks of sexuality. A main thrust of my proposal is that, unlike expressions of sensuality that parents and a culture affirm, expressions of sexuality are born of disapproval, shaming (disgust-revulsion or startle-revulsion), and prohibition. Consequently, a person's expressions of sexuality inevitably involve his or her confrontation with a barrier. The confrontation with the prohibitive barrier may be more or less intense but always involves a degree of edginess and rebelliousness from infancy. The strength of adolescent and adult sexual arousal, desire, or lust gives to sexuality qualities of subversiveness, perniciousness, and transgressiveness. However, for many adolescents, the transgressive trend against childhood and current adult prohibitions is counterbalanced by cultlike trends in peer group sensual and sexual mores. For example, a current trend in adolescent sexuality is the sanctioning of oral sex as a modality for orgasm without penetration or risk of pregnancy. In a large survey of adolescents by the National Center for Health Statistics, more than half had engaged in oral sex. The proportion was equal for males and females and equal for cunnilingus and fellatio.

Adult lovemaking hopefully will include shared sensual pleasure and can be performed with mutual tenderness and empathic sensitivity to the desires of the partner. But, for full arousal, excitement, and orgastic release, those universally affirmed qualities will not be and cannot be all. The joker in the deck lies in qualities of subversion and transgression and perniciousness that give to lust its particular coloration.

I identify three ways in which sexuality in general and heightened arousal in particular are subversive. First, the pleasure of arousal places the individual in conflict with the verdict of authority that defines masturbation, "making out," intercourse, or various highly enjoyable mutual desired practices as bad, forbidden, or evil. When the body sends one message and the prohibitor another, a person may try to believe and accept the authority, but a dissenting voice from within will press to challenge the validity of the authority's dictum. Second, and often more problematic, is the subversion not only of the belief that sexuality is shameful and repulsive but also, under the passion of arousal, for people to become deaf to dangers that are serious, such as unwanted pregnancies, AIDS and other sexually transmitted diseases, being caught in acts of infidelity, and so on. Subversion enters the mix as both a useful challenge to societies' "rational" moralizing and a dangerous challenge to actual serious risks. Third, heightened arousal subverts a wish or requirement to attend to other areas of motivation; the colloquial expression to be "horny" describes the triumph of Eros over all other motivational needs and desires.

The subversion of attention to other motivations can also be described as an outcome of the pernicious nature of lust. By *pernicious*, I refer to the demand of sexual desire to persist until relieved. Society's prescription of a cold shower completely underestimates the power of fantasy, the lure of release, and the omnipresence of exciters on television, in magazines, in ads about anything however distant from overt sexuality. Our society sells not only underwear but also insurance or anything else by making it "sexy." Between the power of fantasy, the responsiveness of the body to hormonal changes, and the ubiquity of exciters and attractors, sexual desire can wax or wane unpredictably and often intensifies when least welcome. A person's sense that he or she cannot control the timing or intensity of arousal is often a source of shame and embarrassment. In addition, in the paradox that constitutes the linking of body sensation and fantasy sexual arousal with shame, revulsion, and embarrassment, the knowledge of one's "uncontrollably" shameful proclivities can itself be a source of arousal.

The most apparent transgressive aspect of sexuality is that each expression of desire involves pushing against cultural restraints inculcated by parents in the child and then reinforced in varied forms by peers, teachers, and religious precepts at any point in life. Pushing against restraints involves varying degrees of assertion and aggression to overcome the prohibition or prohibitor. The aggressive element in sexual expression creates another edge in that not only can it arouse shame and guilt, even revulsion, against the self, but also it may become a source of arousal—the sadomasochistic aspect of both ordinary and pathological forms of sexual expression. Some degree of controlled inflicted or experienced pain in the course of arousal may be another transgressive element. Also, to violate—whether rules, prohibitions, myths of idealized pure love, or the boundaries of another person's body—can be a contributor to heightening excitement. Finally, a sense of abandonment to the excitement of the moment, of going all the way, letting it all hang out, actively spurs the excitement, the wildness of the enactment of the desire.

In these descriptions of subversiveness, perniciousness, and transgressiveness, I have made no attempt to depict the extent with which they color a particular individual's sense of his or her sexuality, only that to some degree they are always present. The intensity of the rebelliousness, aggressiveness, desire to violate, the interference with other motivations, or the denial of risk will certainly affect the individual and his or her partners. Moreover, how much of these "wild card" inclinations are conscious and tolerated, whether the transgressive inclinations operate in fantasy only, are actualized, or are unconscious—either as the repressed dynamic unconscious or as procedural memory—will affect how each partner conducts him- or herself and what they cocreate between them. Those qualities heavily ingrained in one partner's sexuality that he or she cannot accept will often be unconsciously attributed to the other. Fonagy (2006) referred to the aversive unassimilated qualities as "alien" and as dealt with by the individual through projection and projective-identification. Fonagy suggested an analogy between these aspects of sexuality and the disturbed regulation of affects and relationships in borderline states. In my view, at times of high arousal, a fluid boundary between self and partner exists, with rapid transmission of roles and specific desires allowing each partner to use the other to free him- or herself from restraints that would inhibit their path to orgastic release.

In psychoanalysis, sexual subversiveness and transgressiveness have a paradoxical effect of moving the treatment forward. In the cauldron of transference and countertransference, sexuality becomes subversive to the patient's (and analyst's) preexistent beliefs. Once open to question, problematic sexual patterns and strategies can be captured by a spirit of inquiry allowing their necessity and value to be questioned. In psychoanalysis, sexuality is helpfully transgressive in that it provides an intensity and impetus strong enough to break through prior pathological restrictions and patterns of expression and open the erotic imagination and experimentation to access to a richer hedonic intersubjectivity.

CHAPTER 7

Attachment Love, Romantic Love, Lustful Love, Lust Without Love, and Transference Lofe

INTRODUCTION

If love is a many splendored thing, what are its many splendors? How do they come about? In this chapter, I will discuss the origins of love in early development. I will then turn to adult experience and consider the persistence of different strategies of attachment love and how these strategies relate to romantic love and lustful love. The success and persistence of adult love in its many forms comes into question with a roughly 50% divorce rate and the frequency of extramarital affairs. Many pairs (both heterosexual and homosexual) fail in the challenge to persevere in a long experience of a shared monogamous sexually active family life despite a traditional cultural pressure to do so. And many individuals succumb to a life of lust without love. I will consider many of the manifestations of love or its absence that are involved in adult pairings in general and finally in the transference love of treatment dyads.

ATTACHMENT LOVE: ORIGINS

Attachment in its ordinary, nontechnical usage refers to a form of connection between humans that involves symmetric or asymmetric interdependence, commitment, loyalty, and affection cemented by sensual contact. In comparison to the immediacy of the engulfment of romantic passion and love, attachment involves continuity and staying power. Two young people having a passionate affair (romantic and lustful love) decide to live together for several years to test their compatibility over time to remain together (be attached). Two somewhat older professionals live busy lives largely separately but share a deep affectionate commitment to each other. Two elderly people live together in retirement (*On Golden Pond*), and each doubts he or she would live long without the other. I have used as examples pairs who have been heterosexual or homosexual sexual partners, but sisters, brothers, parent and adult child, and friends can also share attachment, affection, and commitment.

All these pairs will offer each other the hug, the affectionate glance, concerned look, and arm over the shoulder that Kohut (1977) recognized as facilitators vitalizing or soothing selfobject experiences.

When attachment is used as a designator of a highly organized, broad-based research method and development theory, love is a rarely addressed concept. Attachment research focuses on seeking the safety of a secure base, and *love*, a complex affect, is difficult to define and research. In the model sequence of strange situation research, the child is initially playing with toys (the affect is interest). The mother leaves once or twice, and the child reacts with distress (crying, fear, and anger) and seeking behavior; the mother returns, picks up the crying child, comforts and restores (the affect is relief) the child, and returns the child to play. However, in the multitude of nondistress moments, mother and child cast love-filled glances at one another, giggle and play joyfully, and evoke the most sensual pleasure of mutual connectedness in each other and in the eyes of any onlooker (immortalized in thousands of paintings of Madonna and child). Kohut's (1977) triad of triggers for selfobject experiences of vitalization or soothing—mirroring, twinship, and idealization—are powerful contributors to mutual affectionate appreciation. Thus, the same strategies for child and mother of seeking, securing, and moving toward that ensure a secure base also ensure an affectionate loving connectedness. Three questions arise:

1. Is the love of a mother and a secure attachment child symbolically represented by the mother as the complex affect we call love, and felt in a form of elemental consciousness by the neonate and young child, the same as, similar to, or categorically different from the love of adult attached pairs?
2. If the securely attached mother and child is the model of an "innocent," uncomplicated "attachment love," what is the status of attachment love in insecurely attached mother–child pairs?
3. Can there be attachment without love, and for some children is their neither attachment nor love?

First, comparing a self-with-other affect state of baby and parent to that of adult partners involves conceptual difficulties. We can attempt an empathic entry into a baby's state of mind based on visual and auditory clues, especially facial expressions and context, while recognizing that the level of consciousness of the baby is qualitatively different. We are aided by the studies of Tomkins (1963) and his followers on categorical affects such as joy, interest, surprise, distress, fear, shame, and anger that appear at birth or within a few months.

In chapter 1, I discussed the argument about whether shame can be inferred in infancy or can be regarded only when self-referencing is possible for the child. The parallel to shame—I did something bad (in my view or my mother's) and I am ashamed of myself—is we get on well together, I love you, and you love me. In this rendering, the child is cognitively processing symbolic representations that are capable of procedural and declarative memory. But, what about before self-referencing and symbolization? Does the beatific smile exchanged between a mother and a 3-month-old qualify as an experience we can call love, or are we accurately reading the mother but adultifying the child? If the 3-month-old's shared smile is not love, what is it? The answer for theorists of the self-referencing persuasion would be that it is joy that is solely an intrapsychic reaction rather than an intersubjective sharing. This argument is rather like the discredited claim that an infant's affects are only reflexes or drive discharges rather than feelings or the old belief that an infant's smiles are only gas. Because I believe that one of the strongest threads we have from birth to death is affective experience, I regard the sparkling positive affective experience of mother and baby to be love, and that love has an essential continuity with the later and more complex childhood, adolescent, and adults forms of love. Lieberman, St. John, and Silverman (2007, p. 258) regarded children's dependence as incorporating a child's sense of "I am aware I need you to look after me in a variety of caretaking ways" with "I need (and love) You." This passionate attachment, the precursor of all intimate relationships and especially of romantic love, lies in the love experienced in the "I need (and love) You."

Second, interest and joy, relief of distress, the satisfaction of a variety of needs, and a sense of safety and security draw (attract) children to seek attachment contact and connection. All children also experience startle, distress, fear, anger, shame, and sadness. In the strange situation protocol, the returning mother of a securely attached child picks the child up and, through comforting, restores the child to a nondistress state of a sense of safety and the ability to return to exploratory play, thereby establishing herself as a secure base. A secure base experience facilitates love; it is not love in itself. The returning mother (or, of course, the mother who never left) can woo her baby into a love exchange by adding the sensual components of the universal patterns of cooing voice tone, gentle touch, skin fondling, and an evocative smile. When I say secure base experiences facilitate love exchanges, I mean that they make it more likely to occur than do insecure attachment experiences. Through their seeking and then pushing off, ambivalently attached children are saying, "I need your presence, comfort, and reassurance, but I did not trust you.

Some of the time, you present me with a security-giving response, and some of the time you are too distracted, angry, depressed, or frightened, and that makes me insecure, fearful, and angry." These children are intensely desirous of reactivating the good experiences with the responsive mother and any moments of loving exchange with her, but they are also wary of which mother may be present. They can be wooed into a loving exchange, but their wariness and anger add a hate side to their loving. Avoidantly attached children's potential for loving exchanges is severely compromised by their desperate strategy to protectively not expose their desire for comfort and reassurance, their anger at the actual and anticipated rejection, and often their overt displays of protest as well. This strategy follows the principle that if the child does not actively seek or even know he or she desires a loving response, the child will not be exposed to an indifferent response or be angrily pushed away. The child can then retain the fantasy and unconscious belief that he or she is loved. Through avoidance of becoming open to desire and the resentment associated with the past rejections, the child can retain the fantasy and unconscious belief that not only is he or she loved, but also, rather than angry, the child is loving. Thus, in the ambivalently and avoidantly attached child love survives but is inextricably coupled with negative affects of fear, anger, shame, and sadness.

Third, attachment without love may be difficult to imagine. Spitz's (1962) study of hospitalism and infants with failure-to-thrive syndrome offers evidence for children who develop neither attachment nor love. Many far less extreme situations may allow for some degree of secure base experience with little or no possibility of affection and sensual sharing. Mothers who are severely depressed or "zoned out" on alcohol and drugs may function in robotic ways like Harlow's (1962) wire monkey mothers, neither giving nor seeking affection. Children who are aggressively traumatized by abuse retain the seeking component of attachment but forgo even the possibility of true affectionate exchanges. My experiences years ago with dangerous criminals in the Baltimore, Maryland, jail system and extensive interviews with delinquent adolescents in a training school, plus other contacts with individuals diagnosed as psychopaths, strongly suggests to me the existence of attachments, sometimes intense, to traumatizing caregivers without love as a past or potential experience.

ROMANTIC LOVE

Jane and Martin meet at a mutual friend's dinner party. They share looks of interest, talk, and recognize the chemistry, the spark between them. Each looks forward to a date that cements their initial impression. They have obstacles—living in different cities, prior obligations, different religions, a disapproving parent—but they overcome them because to be together is heavenly, to be apart is painful. Each talks to friends about the other in excited idealizing terms. They consider commitment, living together, and marriage and swallow their doubts and reservations. Propelled by their excitement—mental and physical—with each other, they marry in a burst of pledges to remain as they are. They hope to sustain the romantic ideal each has of the other and their future together. That is, they hope to beat the odds of the cynics who say it cannot be done.

This "plot" enlivens movies, novels, and television sitcoms in its presumed fulfillment or in dramas like *Romeo and Juliet* in its star-crossed tragic impossibility. We are so familiar with the plot we assume that the essential features of romantic love are universals common to men and women throughout the long history of humankind. Evidence indicates otherwise (de Rougement, 1956; Fiedler, 1966). Our contemporary view (myth) of romantic love began at the end of the 11th century with the troubadour poets. These poets sang of a form of courtly love that valorized the asexual devotion and dedication of a knight to an idealized pure woman—the saintly queen who provided inspiration for his exploits. By the end of the 16th century, the myth of courtly love inspired the story of Sir Walter Raleigh throwing his cloak on the puddle before Queen Elizabeth and the complete parody of it by Cervantes in *Don Quixote*. A form of romantic love, now no longer asexual, came to our age through the romanticism of the English and European novels of the Victorian age. Some novels (many now forgotten) adhered to the purity and inspiring quality of consummated romantic love, and some rebelled openly against its strictures, like the novels of George Sand and Flaubert. Some novels had it both ways, like *Anna Karenina*. Freud, a child of the 19th century, deconstructed the romantic myth by revealing its underpinnings in repressed body origins of oral, anal, and phallic strivings and its childhood versions in the oedipal period. Yet, Freud was a Victorian in his version of what the superego should dictate: Romantic love should ensure the sanctity of nonperverse sexual practices in a monogamous marriage, a marriage that could absorb "ordinary unhappiness" without neurotic symptoms.

In the post-Freudian 20th century, faith in a sanctified lasting romantic commitment could no longer be maintained, but Fiedler (1966) stated:

> We live still, in the Age of the Word (and the cinema which is its child), so that no matter how vulgarized the sentimental myth may have become, no matter how smugly we snicker at it, we are somehow still its victims and beneficiaries. Certainly, there is no one in our world to whom the phrase, "They lived happily ever after," is meaningless or unclear; for us the "happy ending" is defined once and for

all: after many trials, the sacred marriage! Our secure sense of what happiness means in this context has nothing to do with what we *know* about divorce statistics or the possibilities of successful adjustment in marriage; it is a mythological rather than a factual statement. (p. 46)

Although the conviction that the couple will live happily ever after is mythological, the experience of heightened, exciting, romantic love or what we call *infatuation* is factual. Also, although for all couples the thrust of Cupid's arrows will fade with the exigencies of ordinary daily life, for many couples the romantic affective state can be reactivated often with the appropriate props of flowers, gifts, a dinner out, or a weekend at a hotel resort. However, as we examine the story of the historic origins of romantic love, so many pitfalls appear that we can be impressed with the carry power of the desire for the retention of the idealized fantasy. In the poetics of the age of chivalry, the relationship is not of equals but of a totally idealized woman, generally the wife or daughter of an important man. For the courtier, the purity of the idealized beloved must be preserved, or the illusion disappears. Here, we recognize the fantasy of the virginal Madonna that the man cannot have sexually without arousing guilt and shame for defiling, or whose presumed moral superiority arouses his desire to defile as a stimulant to his lust and a source of revenge for being "made" to feel inferior and guilty. But, the idealization-idolatry of women is only one of many fantasies. "The lover may kneel before his mistress, but he kneels not to pledge himself to humility ... but to ask her hand, that is, to become not her servant but her master" (Fiedler, 1966, p. 60). Despite the poetics of the age of chivalry, the actual situation at the time was that men in authority regarded their wives as chattel, young women in their demesne as prey, and daughters as economic property to use to promote position and wealth through marital alliances.

In contemporary courting, power might be considered relatively evenly divided between expression of the man's desire for the woman and the woman's desire for the man. However, power in myths shifts. In the Don Juan myth, the male seducer exploits the woman's gullibility to capture and abandon her. Anthony Trollope noted, "There are men in whose love a great deal of hatred is mixed—who love as the huntsman loves the fox" (from the *Eustace Diamonds*, cited in Glendinning, p. 465). In the myth of the sirens Scylla and Charibides, their songs lure men to death, and in the of myth of Circe, men are seduced to remain with their captor only to be turned into pigs, an ironic twist on the feminist insult of chauvinist pig.

In Bowlby's evolutionary stance, humans are motivated to seek and obtain a secure base at times of danger and loss and to ensure reproduction. Attachment love would be an outcome of having obtained a secure base in adult pairing and a motive to retain it. Lustful love would be a direct route to reproduction. How does romantic love fit into this evolutionary schema? Romantic love in its everyday, down-to-earth form rather than a poetic ideal brings not only minds together but also, importantly, brings bodies together. Down-to-earth romantic love prepares minds and bodies for lustful love. In connecting romantic love to lustful love, I state the obvious, but I hope to offer a less-obvious suggestion: Romantic love establishes sensuality (not primarily sexuality) as a valued experience that holds couples together. Kissing; fondling; holding hands; experiencing the warmth of the two bodies; dressing up; stripping down; exchanging glances; showering together; being playful; competing good naturally; sharing music, art, nature, good jokes, bad jokes, teasing, tickling; and lapsing into silence and a resting state, all link back through affective memory to both dyadic and triadic vitalizing and soothing experiences of childhood. Just as parents need to read the signals of their child for preferences of a host of body responses, the period of romantic coming together facilitates each partner's signaling preferences to the other and each partner's assurance to the other that he or she "gets it." Although the illusory prism of romantic love may obscure the "I know you" of the idealizing partner regarding many characterological qualities, success in the I know you of sensual preferences helps to provide cover and carry power to maintaining an ongoing relationship that always contains an edge of potential divergences.

If sharing knowledge of each other's sensual preferences provides one form of intersubjective vitality to the couple, then the problem of retaining the power to interest and entice the other introduces a challenge to the ongoing relationship when romantic love is not in ascendance. Of course, power in marital relationships can refer to many issues: the power to demand and command; the power of the purse; the power to intimidate, betray, and abandon; the power to encourage and support or depreciate and humiliate. I suggested (chapter 2) that the ability to interest, to captivate, to arouse another is a form of power already appreciated in the romantic love of the 4- to 6-year-old child. In adolescent and adult mutual infatuation and continuing romantic love, the power to excite and hold the interest of the other is more or less equal. Romeo and Juliet were equally desirous of the other despite their torments of loyalty to their respective feuding families or else their dedication at death would lack the compelling tragic ending Shakespeare created. When romantic love is ascendant, life goes on, but no other motive assumes greater significance. In time, many other possible motivations add stress to the pair: "You are married to your work, not me." "You spend so much time driving the children, I never see you." The significance for each gender's enhancing the continued appeal for the other can be appreciated by the economic size of the perfume, after shave lotion, underwear (Victoria's Secret), fashion magazine, and health club industries.

The significance for each gender's enhancing personal continued romantic appeal for the other lies in the omnipresence of a fantasized (and sometimes actual) rival. Inevitably in fantasy and often in actuality, a woman evaluates her mate's attractiveness with that of another potential or actual idealized man, the suitor she did not choose, the husband of her sister or her neighbor who flirts with her, her employer or fellow worker, all probably with some degree of overtones of her father. In addition, in fantasy and often in actuality, a woman evaluates her own attractiveness compared with that of another potential or actual idealized woman, the girl her husband did not choose, the wife of her brother or her neighbor that her husband likes to look at, one or more women her husband works with, all probably with some overtones of her mother. The comparison she makes can reassure or prod her into more effort to make herself appealing or set her off into pangs of jealousy and suspicion.

In comparable fashion, a man can consciously or unconsciously compare his wife's attractiveness to that of his idealized woman. He can use his fantasies of an actual or fantasized woman to evoke romantic fantasies and feelings. His own ability to interest and be attractive will be evaluated against a standard of an actual or fantasized past or present rival, with both idealized woman and rival having probable unconscious linkages to the earlier (4- to 6-year-old) romantic triangular relationships. Kernberg (1995) stated that there are "potentially, in fantasy, always six persons in the bed together, the couple, their respective unconscious oedipal rivals, and their unconscious oedipal ideals" (p. 88). For each person connecting his or her actual relationship with the secret fantasy of the actual or fantasized other may both enhance the romantic moment and be a form of depreciating and betraying the partner. In any case, the secret (or conscious) sensual fantasies of the idealized other introduces an inevitable tension and a potential conflict involving shame and guilt into romantic love. Likewise, secret (or conscious) fantasies about the rival introduce into romantic love a degree of inevitable apprehension and a potential conflict of jealousy and suspicion.

ADULT ATTACHMENT LOVE

Kohut (1977) used a quotation from Eugene O'Neill, "The Grace of God is glue," to refer to Tragic Man's need for selfobject experiences to mend his broken (fragmented) sense of self through human connectedness. For adult partners to remain together, I believe attachment love is that glue. Romantic love, with its infatuation, preoccupation with the loved one, sensual pleasures and longings, and idealizations of both the loved one and the emotional drama of the state itself (accompanied by a heightened level of amphetamine-like substances; Eagle, 2007), brings the couple together (other than in arranged marriages). When the sentimental myth of "and they lived happily ever after" meets the grind of daily life, ranging from competition over resources to bathroom smells, something has to go. Either the couple splits, each to search for a new partner to revive the myth, or the myth is surrendered, and the satisfaction of passion and dreams is replaced by the cooler sustaining affects of safety and security (accompanied by endorphin release similar to that of infant–mother affectionate bonds; Eagle, 2007). Eagle cited evidence that about 2 years are regarded for proximity seeking, separation protest, and safe haven and secure base to come fully into play in a romantic relationship. Placed on a time line, attachment love based on familiarity and security provides a background connection over long periods during which romantic love and lustful love (hopefully) make frequent foreground entries, adding spice and spirit to the couple's life together.

Attachment and romantic love have similarities that enable each to blend into the other. Each partner brings into their romantic and attachment love a long history of shared sensual experiences dating to infancy. Based on procedural memory, eyes know to look and meet; hands to reach to touch, fondle, and stroke; lips to meet; bodies to move toward, all providing reassurance of the responsiveness of the other. Fantasies elaborate what the body perceives about the sensual state of self and other. Sensitive empathic awareness of the partner allows an adult to discriminate between when the sensual connection indicates a need for security and when the sensual connection indicates an upsurge of romantic feelings.

Along with the sensual components that provide continuity between attachment and romantic love are disagreements that inevitably disrupt the harmony of any intimate relationship. On the romantic side, lover's spats arise over the relative strength of affection and commitment, the availability for sexuality, and jealous indications of wandering eyes and interest. On the attachment side, couples argue about safety and risk ("You drive too fast," "You didn't buckle the children in tight enough," "You'll spend us into bankruptcy"); neatness and order ("You never put the cap back on the toothpaste," "Your papers are all over the house," "Your hair is a mess"); choice of entertainment, and so on. These disagreements of intimacy sometimes add spice to the relationship but often test the capacity of the couple to repair and restore goodwill regardless of the outcome of the specific argument. Repair and restoration depend on the capacity of each partner to give empathic recognition to the state of mind of the other, to be self-reflective (especially in cooler moments), to acknowledge error, to apologize for causing undue distress, and to avoid becoming stuck in polarized concretized positions and unwarranted ad hominum attacks. Consequently, the success of efforts at repair and restoration of disruptions of romantic and attachment love depends on the existence of prior strategies of secure or insecure attachment and the ability to utilize self-reflection and mentalization.

Both partners who bring to their union strategies for a secure attachment know how to use proximity to gain a sense of safety and to use distance to ensure the opportunity to pursue nonintimate separate or shared motivations, interests, and goals. But, attachment strategies that retain, repair, and restore attachment love are more than internal working models from infancy; the strategies are refined, altered, and added to in response to the challenges of all forms of intimacy encountered in each phase of development. The ability to trust, to communicate coherently, to create a positive sustaining ambiance, and to appreciate context are four qualities that develop from early attachment love and contribute to a smooth back-and-forth transition between attachment and romantic love.

Attachment research distinguishes between the coherent communicative style of securely attached adults and the preoccupied or avoidant–dismissive or chaotic–disorganized communication styles of insecurely attached adults. Working with couples often reveals difficulties in communication that work to create a troubled ambiance that often worsens over time. Mrs. T. called for an appointment for herself and her reluctant husband. Mrs. T. immediately detailed the problems they had with their daughter and Mr. T.'s failure to pay bills and his disappearance at night into an alcoholic haze. She made direct eye contact and appeared to be searching for my reassurance and, in the absence of my affirmation, looked hurt. Mr. T., a large man, sat immobile, looked away, and until addressed directly seemed dissociated. When asked to consider a statement of Mrs. T., he responded with a terse expression of dismissive denial and a condescending smirk. Mrs. T. responded instantly to the provocation with an angry flurry as Mr. T. retreated into an expressionless avoidant posture.

This brief vignette of the communicative problem of the avoidantly attached husband and preoccupied, ambivalently attached wife represents a common pairing (although the genders may well be reversed). The preoccupied partner is desperately seeking reassurance of the affection and esteem of her partner to help her resolve her anxious doubts. Greeted with his lack of response, she increases her attempts to engage, becoming strident and "nagging"—all guaranteed to feed his inclination to seek safety in withdrawal, punish her with his passivity and denial, and anger her with his condescending smirk. As she revs up her distress and protest, she experiences shame and humiliation at her loss of control and an increased sense of righteous indignation at being put in this position. As he responds to her "hysteria," he sadistically enjoys his image of her making a fool of herself, increasing his contempt and disdain and his sense of righteous indignation at her nagging and barraging. A paradoxical feature of this combustible mix is that Mr. and Mrs. T. are strongly "attached" in their problematic mutual dependency. However, attachment and romantic love are placed at greatest risk by the parallel existence of contempt-disdain and shame-humiliation reinforced through the entitlement of righteous indignation. Sincere efforts to repair disruptions and restore affection by one partner often fail to overcome the chronic harboring of resentment by the other partner, often the more silent, avoidant dismissive one.

A man in his 70s, married for 40 years, used his basement office as a "hide-hole" where he could go and "enjoy a good sulk" when his wife criticized his appearance, clothes, or weight. While claiming how much he loved her (they were strongly interdependently attached), he "paid her back" by refusing to attend or enjoy events that were central to her career.

> There is nothing perhaps so generally consoling to a man as a well-established grievance; a feeling of having been injured, on which his mind can brood from hour to hour, allowing him to plead his won case in his own court, within his own heart—and always to plead it successfully." (Trollope, 1992, p. 12)

Returning to the positive aspect of attachment love, many successful couples refer to themselves as best friends. This source of affection draws on the type of relationship common to middle childhood and adolescence (chapter 6). Anthropologists note that in many primates grooming is the activity that cements "friendship"—a demonstration of goodwill and mutual security. Anthropologists have also made the evocative suggestion that the human equivalent of primate grooming is gossiping. Shakespeare referred to an intimate person as "gossip," as in "She's my dear gossip." My point is that gossiping together provides intimacy to couples who talk to one another about friends, relatives, dinner guests, television or movies, or political stars—"What's new?" "Who did you see today?"—all this plus a private world of their view of people, their special confidences. And, beyond the sharing of gossip and views of the here and now, attached couples create a mythlike narrative of their relationship—how they met, where they have been, where they plan to go, when their children were born, who is the social one, who is the shy one—until each can finish the other's sentence in both the telling of old or new stories. My reference to gossip and a shared narrative myth may appear to be too superficial, too surface conscious to be a meaningful component of attachment love. Rather than superficial time filler, I believe the building of a shared narrative, like the creation of an autobiography narrative of themselves and their family by oedipal period children (chapter 2), has deep unconscious roots in adding a rich symbolic connectedness to the affective procedured patterns that couples and families develop. The power of the absence of the other to share the narratives becomes apparent in the specifics of what sets off mourning sadness when one member of a marital pair dies.

I began this discussion suggesting that attachment love is the glue that holds couples together as romantic love (and lustful love) waxes and wanes. Culture and society provide many outlets for attachment love to remain intact while romantic love (or lustful love) is activated in other outlets. Victorian novels portray a society with an upper class that strongly condemned divorce while institutionalizing country house weekends that provided opportunities for flirtations and affairs. Operas from Mozart's *Marriage of Figaro*, to Strauss's *Fliedermaus* celebrate the joys, complications, and risks of splitting attachment and romantic love. The movie *The Captain's Paradise* has Alec Guiness with a conservative, mannered wife in his ship's home port and his wild, exciting mistress in his North African port of call. The paradox central to the plot is his dissatisfaction with what attracts him to each and his converting each woman to be more like the other.

The institutionalizing of mistresses, courtesans, and geishas caters to the illusion of the "sanctity" and stability of attachment love while providing an alternative expression of romantic love. A moralistic conception of the institutions of mistresses, courtesans, and geishas regards them as catering primarily to male lust, comparable to prostitution, only more "classy." I believe a careful examination of these institutions for male expression points to an escape into a world closer to romantic fantasy than simple erotic lust. Katherine Frank, herself a dancer, conducted extensive research on regular customers of strip clubs, and the research resulted in a series of publications. Unlike clubs where men went to have orgasms from lap dancing, erotic massage, or direct sexual contact with the performers, strip clubs require "dancers to keep at least one foot of space between themselves and the customers during dances. Customers were not allowed to touch the dancers, or to touch or expose their own genitals. These rules were rarely openly transgressed, and when they were, the customers were usually asked to leave the club" (2005, p. 487). The interviewees, all regular customers, were heterosexual, educated, middle-class men ranging in age from 28 to 57. In the interviews, the men professed love for their wives and a commitment to monogamy. They also described the loss of their initial romantic passion with their wives. They complained of boredom with their wives' conservative approach to sex and more broad interactions. Their motivations for going to the clubs included a desire to interact with women who were not "feminists" or conservatives. They sought an ego boost from safe interactions without risk of rejection. They liked that they were seen by other men, who witnessed their viral attention to attractive women. They were curious to know a woman in an adventurous, sexualized situation and to engage with her in a transgressive mutual construction of fantasy.

> Dancers offered an opportunity to talk to women with whom these men would not generally be able to interact, for a number of reasons—a lack of attractiveness, age differences, class differences (in either direction), availability, and the women's willingness to interact outside of the clubs, for example. It was not *just* the presence of nudity, nor *just* the presence of talk, that made these venues appealing, but the presence of *both* of these that allowed for the mutual creation of fantasies that were both relaxing and stimulating to the customers. (p. 492)

The primary illusion they sought was the possibility of an intimate, exciting, transgressive sexual relationship without having to act on it. Frank concluded that the men's behavior was

> *transgressive* through its *sexualization* (though without sexual contact or release) and its proscription, and *sexualized* through its *transgressiveness*. The excitement of the visits was experienced in the context of relationships in which a conservative woman would find this behavior upsetting and would feel betrayed or hurt if she knew about it. (p. 498)

This made keeping the visits secret a future exciting form of transgression.

This type of paid-for stripping, nudity, and erotic dancing with no touching allowed is portrayed by Natalie Portman as the dancer in a strip club scene in the movie *Closer*. The dancing and stripping in the private room are extremely erotic, but the male is not an admirer or a regular but an angry, vengeful man and the sexy female a deeply unhappy woman.

Although Dr. Frank's studies are based on clubs where the strippers are female and the clients males, male strip clubs for female clients also exist. One venue has gender-specific clubs on each floor of the same building.

I present Dr. Frank's research on regular strip club customers to illustrate how one group of married men arranged to preserve attachment love with their spouses. These men remained "faithful" in their own minds by not having extramarital orgasms like men or women who had mistresses or lovers. They were not men who went to prostitutes or to clubs where arrangements for orgasms, like lap dancing, masturbation, or direct sexual contact, were performed or made. Nonetheless, these men were secretly rebelling against the actual or presumed strictness of their "conservative" prohibiting wives and enjoying the erotic excitement of subverting the constraints they had or imagined from her and society. When examined in the light of the transgressive nature of their behavior and fantasies, we move from attachment love into the realm of lustful love experiences.

LUSTFUL LOVE

To a pure romantic, lustful love is an oxymoron. If lust means bodies drawn to one another in states of erotic excitement for the purpose of orgasmic release, then to a pure romantic that constitutes animalistic passion, not love. If lust means that in the fantasies of each of the lustful pair, the image of the other shades away from an idealized respectful portrayal of the other into subversive notions of the other as wild and passionate, then to a pure romantic that is debasement and dehumanization, not love. If lust means that the excitement states of one or both of the lustful pair is intensified by inclusion of elements of pain, aggressive thrusting, and fantasies that include assertions of power, then to a pure romantic that is anger, sadism, or masochism, not tenderness and love. If lust means that one or both of the pair add to their excitement by actions or fantasies that violate some past or present socially accepted propriety, then to a pure romantic, some religious groups, and some psychoanalytic theories, the transgressive lustful lovers are pathologically perverse, not guided by the correct ordering of foreplay and genital primacy.

In actual practice, lustful love generally includes some or all of these deviations from a romantic ideal. Furthermore, the deviation in itself heightens the excitement. Lustful love is about bodies, rising and falling sensations, sweat, smells, and secretions. Lustful love is about minds turned loose to erotic imagination in which love and respect mix with possessiveness and domination. Caring deeply about the other mixes with moments of caring only about the pleasures of the self. Distinct awareness of self with other mix with moments in which boundaries of the self identity and the identity of the other can become confused, reversed, and fused. Playfulness and spontaneity mix with familiarity, repetition, and engrossment. By referring to bodies and minds as if separate entities, I make an artificial incorrect separation. In lustful love, a lover's experience may be that his or her body turns on his or her erotic imagination, or the lover's experience may be that the erotic imagination triggers the body into an arousal state. Or, her body may excite his imagination or body, and his arousal may stimulate her body and fantasy. That description may fit the manner in which the lustful lovers experience the origins of their states of arousal, but physiologically lustful excitement is never as linear. The interplay of two individuals' neural networks and transmitters, hormonal and genital vascular engorgement, on self-regulation and mutual regulation occurs with the simultaneous melding of the multiple influences. Cues and clues regarding who leads and who follows operate at rates too rapid to be conscious. The simultaneous interplay is based on implicit knowing and unconscious anticipation, expectation, and responsiveness.

To continue my emphasis on the inevitability subversive and transgressive elements in sexuality, I have contrasted lustful love with the myth of a "pure" romantic ideal. I now describe the carryover of both attachment and romantic love into the lustful love of two securely attached individuals. In my discussion of a securely attached couple, I am assuming each partner recognizes the other as a center of desire rather than a traditional bias of male desire and domination and a female devoid of desire who submits to domination. From attachment love, each partner can carry into sexual arousal the security of knowing the other is reliably available when need or danger arises. From romantic love, each partner can carry into sexual arousal the pride each feels in existence as the chosen one of the other.

Safety and pride are important in making the transition from the security each may have in arousing affirmation when all dressed up at a party to the much greater risk of naked bodies with their imperfections. The "naked" self and other as he and she might be more objectively seen are often altered in the erotic imagination to be more suitable for the arousal needs of one or both. The coloration of self and other may be borrowed from a memory of a more romantic time between them (she before her figure changed with babies, he before his paunch) or borrowed from a movie star, a Victoria's Secret ad, or a mutually enjoyed "porn flick." The image of self and other may be altered to be more patient or more turned on, more cool and suave or more hot and "dirty," more a subtle seducer, or more a "hotty." These fantasized attributions about the self and other are moderate realignments of images that have the potential to enhance arousal and pleasure and move self and other toward enacting desired roles. A great benefit of each partner's feeling safe to project onto the self and the other a role that enhances the success of their experience during lustful love is that, in a postcoital period, the couple can reactivate romantic love through an idealization of the experience.

Just as in romantic love, "in lustful love reciprocity is key. If sexual excitement is generated through increasing awareness of the excitement of the other, then genuine desire on both sides is essential. Of course, this is not always the case" (Fonagy, 2005). Excitement registers broadly across the body, in the eyes, face, posture, gesture, movement, and genitals. For each gender, the indicator of the excitement of the other is equally recognizable except for the genitals. The erect penis is far more discernible than the woman's perineal engorgement and vaginal lubrication. Consequently, women can be adept at providing men with the illusion of reciprocity by compliant behavior and faked orgasm.

Mikulincer and Shaver (2007) suggested ways in which strategies of insecure attachment influence lustful love. Lovers with preoccupied attachment patterns tend to become overcentered on sexual performance. In their overemphasis, they may make coercive attempts to push a partner into having sex. They may hypervigilantly monitor their partner's signals of arousal, attraction, and rejection to regulate their heightened concerns about attractiveness and their ability to gratify and hold on to their partner. In contrast, avoidant dismissive attachment strategies play out sometimes as inhibited sexual desire and avoidance of sexual contact. Another avoidant pattern is a shallow cynical disparaging of the partner and divorcing of sexual activity from kindness and intimacy. Still another pattern that can develop from the avoidant attachment strategy is a narrow focus on orgastic pleasure, promiscuity, and self-aggrandizing "conquests."

Mikulincer and Shaver (2007) pointed out the importance of secure attachment for both attachment love and lustful love. They noted that positive sexual relations with the same partner require high doses of physical closeness, potential vulnerability, and personal disclosure. People who are relatively secure are open to be attentive to signals of sexual arousal and attraction and to perceive a partner's interest accurately. Thus, compared with insecurely attached people, lustful lovemaking of securely attached partners does not emphasize or depend on coercion, exploitation, hypervigilant monitoring, emotional distancing, domination, submission, self-aggrandizing, conquering, and a focus on personal orgasm at the expense of mutual satisfaction. However, given the transgressive aspect I believe is inherent in all lustful love, some loss of perfect respect for and consideration of the partner as in the list in the preceding sentence enters into (but does not dominate) successful orgastic arousal states of each participant.

For authentic long-lasting lustful love, a high degree of reciprocity is key not only to the success of the lust but also to the success of the love. The love in erotic excitement and its physical expression may be described by several statements, including (a) I love the pleasure it gives me, (b) I love your enjoyment and appreciation of the pleasure I give you, (c) I lovingly sense you and respond to you, and (d) I recognize that your individuality makes the reciprocal love meaningful to me. When either partner locks into his or her own pleasure and the mirroring of his or her own pleasure states as experienced by the other, lustful love becomes love only in the narcissistic sense. Intersubjective lustful love requires oscillation between those narcissistic pleasures and the subjective state of the other before, during, and after "love" making.

Just as reciprocity or the illusion of it is key to becoming and maintaining arousal, intimacy with multiplicity in the gendered self is key to recognizing and appreciating the subjectivity of the partner through an awareness of opposite-gendered desires in the self. My clinical observation suggests that in lovemaking women more than men can sense themselves into the gender-tinged duality of active-passive, entering-entered, and separate-fused. Traditional, cultural values have placed greater pressure on men to repress and deny their feminine desires to preserve a macho illusion needed to maintain their arousal. Both men and women can experience lustful love as precarious because of the fluidity of boundaries, especially at moments of maximal excitement and release. Accordingly, the cohesiveness of the sense of self, of "I a man" or "I a woman," permits men and women to more fully participate in lustful love without threat of loss of autonomy. The challenge for any individual is to integrate his or her opposite-gendered desires into a cohesive sense of self.

I was struck by a lacuna in my knowledge of the symbolism of female orgastic experience when I attended a clinical presentation of the analysis of a woman whose repetitive sexual activities had elements suggestive of addictive dysregulation. At one point, she described a dream that she and her analysis indicated as a transformative shift in self-recognition and self-regulation. In the dream, a herd of large animals in her bedroom was moving in perfect controlled fluid synchrony. Their remarkable activity was known only to the dreamer and experienced as both outside and inside her. As I puzzled unsuccessfully over the imagery that made up the dream, a female member of the group stated as a simple matter of fact that the images referred to a female orgasm. I thought, that makes sense—the particular undulating rhythm, the excited control of a powerful force right on the edge of ability to be controlled. Only the experiencer could know it was happening because it was inside the "bedroom," but for her it was also outside as she looked at herself. She was both experiencer of her internal state and observer of herself experiencing.

A truism states that no person can ever fully appreciate the experience of another, and this applies even more so to gender-specific experiences. However, knowledge helps, and I realized that in my training as physician, psychiatrist, and psychoanalyst, I was never taught anything about the physiology of female orgasmic experience. In the book *She Comes First*, dedicated to teaching men how best to stimulate women before and after coitus to enhance the likelihood of their female partner's orgasmic experience, Kerner (2004) wrote the following:

> The innate biological capacity to achieve multiple orgasms has much to do with the how women, subsequent to orgasm, experience the resolution and return to the prearousal state. Men lose their erections quickly and go into what's called a refractory period (an interval of time that needs to pass before he can get an erection again), but a woman's genitals take far longer to return to their normal state, at least 5 to 10 minutes. Additionally, the clitoris does not contain a venous plexus, the mechanics in the penis for retaining blood and sustaining an erection—a critical element in the explosive male orgasm and the process of insemination. (pp. 175–176)

Kerner's book is a paean to the excitement men can generate for women through stimulation of the clitoris by tongue and touch. The author's point is that because women can have multiple orgasms, precoital clitoral stimulation sets a woman up for maximal enjoyment.

Arguing against the binary portrayal of either pathological clitoral or healthy vaginal orgasm of traditional Freudian theory, Dimen (2003) asked why choose when women can have both:

> The problem, and solution, is that no single organ represents Woman's desire (much less anyone's). There really is no Queen to partner King Phallus. ... Women don't want just the genitals. They, we, want whatever is erotic. ... (Wo)man can, want, and do have both clitoral and vaginal orgasms, maybe not the same woman, maybe not at the same time, maybe not each time, and maybe alternately or simultaneously, with other climaxes, like those of the "G-spot" (Whipple & Komisaruk, 1991) or anus ... who knows? (p. 60)

Parallel to a continuum of orgasmic possibilities for women, Dimen cited the continuum for men of orgasm without semen expulsion, typical ejaculatory orgasm, and nonejaculatory emission. "Whatever is erotic" of course includes breasts and nipples when viewed, stroked, or sucked; mouth and tongue; legs viewed, kissed, or stroked; ears when blown into; any skin area when bitten gently; and any body parts from toes to hair that in the imagination of any pair acts as a "turn-on."

The different physiology of male and female genitals helps to explain common complaints of lovemakers. The woman's slower, more protected, arousal state calls for an extended period of sensual and sexual arousal for a full pleasurable experience. The man's more rapid erection tends him to a more rapid, less-patient, desire for heightened excitement and release. During coitus, both can increase their excitement pleasure by prolonging the period before his ejaculation, an adjustment calling for sensitivity of the male for his partner's state. Postejaculation, men rapidly enter a spent state, but woman can continue to enjoy an arousal state if some form of stimulation continues.

Attachment strategies can have a direct impact on the success or failure of lustful love. Securely attached partners are open to read each other's signals and to communicate verbally about these desires for and from the other. An avoidantly attached man is likely to be desirous only of his orgasmic experience, neither preparing his partner well nor maintaining interest in her after ejaculating. Her desires before, during, and after are apt to be dismissed, sometimes coldly, arrogantly, and contemptuously. Avoidantly attached women frequently experience somatic symptoms: the classic headache and tiredness that serves to avoid a lustful experience or the discomfort or pain that during coitus interferes with full arousal. A preoccupiedly attached man may become so focused on whether his partner is having an orgasm, whether he is able to satisfy her, that his nagging, unrecognized demands on her to reassure him act as deadeners of real passion for both. A preoccupation that affects lustful love can be focused on anything any obsessional fear or revulsion can fix on: smells, dirt, disease, pregnancy, injury, jealousy, envy. My clinical experience indicates that whatever specific preoccupation many women fix on that affects their lustful love, an underlying concern of these insecurely attached women is whether they are really loved or their body is being used. Caught in this dilemma, many women, desperate to assure themselves of being loved, submit to sexual practices or frequency they do not personally desire. Consequently, just as in a caretaker reversal solution to ambivalent attachment in childhood, they become both subservient in behavior and deeply resentful, leading to passive–aggressive approaches to both attachment and lustful love.

Lustful lovemaking lends itself to being regarded as a performance and that perspective opens a path to problems since performance means exposure to failure in the eyes of the performer or the other. Performance also means playing a role like stud or sexy babe. For both genders to perform in lustful love means to be transgressive in some manner, and problems arise when the shame, guilt, or fear about transgressiveness prevent performance. The initial problem is shame, guilt, or fear causing the failure in performance, and the subsequent problem is the paralyzing shame, embarrassment and humiliation resulting from the failure to perform. For men, impotence, premature ejaculation, and worries about penis size have traditionally been related to oedipal period carryovers of shame or guilt about soiling the saintly "immaculate" mother and fear of her protector/possessor, to danger from her soil and disease, or to the threat of her aggressive Medusa snakes or vagina dentate. Although these emasculating threats have been identified for over a century, Giddens (1992) believed that the sociological change from women's rise to economic, political, and attitudinal parity has moved the balance from shame and guilt over despoiling the virginal female mother stand-in to fear of a no-longer-dominated woman's demand for intimacy and equality in a true intersubjective relationship. "Many men are unable to construct a narrative of self that allows them to come to terms with an increasingly democratized and reordered sphere of personal life" (p. 117).

For generations, women have been warned by their mothers not to be too smart, assertive, and ambitious or they will scare men away. Now, many women are caught in a paradox. Many contemporary men desire intelligent and productive women as mates but in lustful love may require their mate to be compliant with the up-and-down rhythm of the penis rather than the fully deserved intimacy and prolonged lovemaking women's rhythm requires. Of course, outside these broad sociological forces are well-recognized specific developmental influences on female lustful performance.

Nancy (Lichtenberg, Lachmann, & Fosshage, 1996) began her analysis suffering from genital anesthesia resulting from repression of sensation as her accommodation to her brother's masturbating against her body. Nancy had accepted the indoctrination from her father, mother, and brother that she and women were temptresses whose dangerous sexuality aroused and corrupted men.

Mary Jane, the patient mentioned in chapter 1 whose presentation of the photograph of sadomasochistic practice with needles evoked my Eew! response, was sexually seduced by a trusted family friend as a young teenager. As an older teenager, she became promiscuous but experienced coitus as painful and never really enjoyed the orgasmic experience until late in her treatment.

Nancy's anesthesia and Mary Jane's vaginal pain interfered with their successful performances, but the narrative of another patient told a different story. This woman, who had also had a seductive childhood experience with a relative, complained bitterly about her husband's sexual demands, especially those for her to perform fellatio at odd times of the day. As she became more able to assert her desires and point of view in many different situations, I asked about her remaining complaint to these particular demands. A "performance" dream helped us to recognize that, despite some embarrassment, she was proud of the skill and expertise of her technique at fellatio.

Returning from the single-case study examples, many complaints about the performance of men and women can be associated with failures to recognize their disparate physiology. Male nonrecognition or denial of women's need for more gradual arousal leads men to claim that the woman is cold and unreceptive and women to claim that all men want to do is "fuck." Another version is the woman's desire for romantic talk, a sensual setting, and a slower physical warm-up; men may fear that so much delay will cause the loss of erection. Another performance issue arises from the value taken from the general desirability of concurrent arousal to a requirement to have concurrent orgasms. The presumption is that the model of ejaculation is the same for both sexes, a phallocentric view that gives primacy to ejaculation and diminishes the value of women's potential for multiple orgasms. This belief can easily lead to either the man believing he is a failure if he cannot get his partner to "come" at the same time as he does or the woman believing she is a failure because her different orgastic experience does not live up to his and her expectations. This problem was dramatized in a *Seinfeld* episode in which Seinfeld, to reassure himself about his performance, reminded Elaine about the many orgasms she had had with him, exemplified by her loud exclamations. "Fake!" she said. "Fake?" he asked in a shocked voice. "Fake, fake, fake," she announced, "All of them fake!"

Another complaint about performance is the postejaculation turnoff by men at a point when woman remain aroused and desirous. Here, the proverbial "what do you want from me, I have a headache" initial female refusal is paralleled by the "what do you want from me, I'm exhausted and half asleep" posterection male refusal.

Prostitutes play a particular role in relieving men of the legitimate complaints by women of the male's failure to establish a loving precoital warm-up and to remain involved after ejaculation. With a prostitute, a man does not have to worry about pleasing the woman with his performance; his pocketbook and the rhythm of his penis rule. In fact, performance success with a prostitute for men depends on at least the illusion of a relationship and the prostitute's success in creating a setting for arousal. In the movie *Never on Sunday*, Melina Mercouri plays a prostitute in Piraeus who is beloved by the town's businessmen and sailors. A young, inexperienced sailor, pressed by his friends to have sex with her, cannot overcome his shyness and shame. In an endearing way, she ends the failed effort, puts him at ease by chatting with him, and creates a sensual ambiance. Relaxed, beginning to experience a relationship with her, the sailor sees her as a responsive, desirous, and desirable woman, and his arousal follows naturally.

Pornography, a huge industry, was largely restricted to the domain of men to excite their desire but has become increasingly exploited by couples to enhance their joint arousal and act as an external source of needed refreshing variety. Giddens (1992) noted:

Heterosexual pornography displays an obsessive concern with standardized scenes and poses in which the complicity of women, substantially dissolved in the actual social world, is reiterated in an unambiguous way. ... In the visual content of pornographic magazines, female sexuality is neutralized, and the threat of intimacy dissolved. The gaze of the woman is normally directed at the reader. ... The male who looks on to this gaze must by definition dominate it. (p. 119)

Giddens continued that the sexual pleasure portrayed is not the male's but the female's ecstasy "under the swag of the phallus. Women whimper, pant and quiver, but the men are silent, orchestrating the events" (p. 120). Frank's (2005) point in her research on strip club regulars and Gidden's point on the use of pornography are that they serve primarily to restore experiences and images of male dominance, thereby rescuing men from the threat of the sociological change of female equality. Gidden's analysis notwithstanding, couples who enjoy the stimulation of shared pornography can, through the plasticity of erotic imagination, use it to create whatever fantasy drama fits their particular needs to enhance their lustful love. Pornography (voyeurism), like variant sexual practices, adds the stimulation of transgressing social "propriety" and prohibition.

LUST WITHOUT LOVE

In prior chapters, I avoided the use of the term *perversion* because for me it has no clear meaning. When the only accepted goal of sexuality was regarded to be reproduction, any sexual practice that did not lead to that outcome could be defined as a perversion of evolution's or God's true purpose. With lustful love liberated from the goal of reproduction by less need for children as workers, the advent of contraception, the frequency of premarital and extramarital sex, gay and lesbian coupling, and family planning, which practice of lustful love can be definitely regarded as perversion? A person might use his or her Eew! factor to define what he or she regards as beyond the pale, indecent, or immoral. In a sociological situation in which male–female relationships are of equals, and each person's subjectivity and desire are recognized and respected by the other, then consensually accepted sexual practices, whether procreative or not, cannot be regarded as perverse in a psychoanalytic "diagnostic" sense. The historic list of sadomasochism, fetishism, mutual masturbation, voyeurism, exhibitionism, transvestism, and homosexuality, when practiced as a consensual choice between two sensitive, caring individuals, constitutes an expression of sexual desire compatible with attachment and romantic love. Playing at power, say in a sadomasochistic script that can shift between which partner has it and which does not, is within lustful love; angrily, violently, vengefully wielding sexual power is lust without love. The key words that differentiate are playful, sensitive, recognizing and respecting the subjectivity and desire of the other, and equality and consensuality of choice.

Sexualized violence against women has a long history. Rape, gang rape, serial killing, politically inspired rape as in Darfur, erotic arousing battering, even cannibalism and necrophilia have been personified in such characters as Jack the Ripper and Bluebeard and portrayed in movies with characters like Hannibal Lecter in *The Silence of the Lambs* and in the Count Dracula series. This historical background provides a context from which to evaluate Gidden's (1992) claim that "a large amount of male sexual violence now stems from insecurity and inadequacy rather than from a seamless continuation of patriarchal dominance. Violence is a destructive reaction to the waning of the female complicity" (p. 122). In my view, contemporary sexual violence may be spurred by the waning of female compliance, but that can only be one source of a long historical playing out of violence between the sexes. Lachmann (2000), building on Kohut's (1972) concept of narcissistic rage following traumatic self-injury and attachment research's findings of the lasting effect of unresolved trauma, pointed to childhood developmental contributions to loss of love and intimacy and an upsurge of eruptive aggression. Women may be the source, the target, and the perpetrator of the hatred that fuel sexual violence. Perfidy and betrayal by men is a factor in woman's eruptive aggression (Medea) whether the perpetrators are fathers or brothers in childhood or destructive relationships in later life.

The examples of lust without love that commonly confront psychoanalysts and psychotherapists are less dramatic but no less problematic to the individuals involved. A woman in her late 20s would frequent bars where strangers would pick her up. Desperately seeking love, she would fantasize that the man was deeply caring and then felt aroused. But, as he came on to her sexually, she would invariably conclude that he only wanted her body, and in her disappointment and hurt would go through a coital performance without either lust or love.

Jacob's (chapter 1) sexual arousal combined desire, stirred originally by his beautiful mother, with his hatred of what he experienced as his mother's cold, self-centered indifference to him. His date rape of a girl at college reflected lust without love, but clearly with hatred. The episode I described that evoked my Eew! response represented his dissociative denial of his affection for his current girlfriend and her for him, leaving him trapped by his loveless lust powered by hate.

Karl had married into a wealthy family despite his wife's parent's objections. At times, she was receptive to his advances, especially when he won her affection by being a good father to their children. At other times, a business setback or a social faux pas would activate her contempt and sensual–sexual rejection. Karl would then go cruising in a search for a male prostitute. Karl described the episodes as finding the prostitute, gesturing to him to get in the car, then (without saying a word) having the prostitute perform fellatio, paying him off, and leaving. This compulsively anonymous sex—clearly lust without love—of having a man "bow" before him at Karl's majestic gesture functioned for Karl to confirm the worth and power of his penis/masculinity.

TRANSFERENCE LOVE

Stimulated by Friedman (2006), Smith (2006) asked, "Is it true that the analyst's love is an illusion and the patient's love 'merely virtual'?" (p. 685). Smith added that, "In his paper on transference love, Freud (1915) famously waffled on whether love in analysis was as genuine as any other love" (p. 685). Freud advised analysts to treat the patient's love as something unreal. Freud's advice is essentially for analysts to dissemble, that is, to respond to an experience that is sensed as genuine as though it is unreal—a protection against the analyst's loss of objectivity, neutrality, and especially abstinence. Friedman defined *virtual* as having a specific psychoanalytic meaning. The exposure of

> the paradox of the past inside the present. ... When people talk to one another, their responses constantly reassure each other that "yes ... it's just me you're talking to, and, of course, it's right now that you're talking." That is precisely what analysts don't say; in fact, not saying it is half their job. That cruel stepping back exposes the noncontemporaneousness of the patient. And it is the unaccustomed spotlight on the person's noncontemporaneousness—his not-all-her-and-not-all-there-ness—that makes the contemporary drama feel only virtual. (pp. 204–205)

Smith's (2006) question contrasts with Friedman's (2006) exposition. Smith asked about both the analyst's and the patient's love; Friedman asked only about the patient's. Friedman explicitly eschewed the contemporary focus on intersubjectivity and coconstructed reality as attempts to normalize the analytic dialogue to be similar to all other human communication. Having established this significance for him of the traditional intrapsychic focus as a means of elaborating the influence of the archaic past (what he calls the monster), Friedman stated that, in our ordinary use of different approaches in clinical practice, "The *proportion* of the ingredients is crucial" (p. 710; italics in original). In considering the different forms of love I have described, I believe the "ingredient" of the analyst's love can never be omitted. I do not believe any patient ever omits it.

Well into an ongoing analysis, a woman patient described herself as sexually aroused and invited me to join her on the couch to "make love." Her "irritation" grew more strident and demanding. As her anger mounted, she mixed seductive cooings with contemptuous reflections on my lack of manhood. I know that she had had an affair with a married analyst colleague. Her mixed pride and guilt had been long under our consideration. Also long under our consideration were origins of her sexual "entitlement" in her childhood and adolescent relations with her father. I also knew she was as fundamentally fond and trusting of me as I was of her, so I believed we had a well-established attachment love. I viewed her state of arousal and her invitation and insistence as both transference (which is an emergent expectation) and real, not an illusion, not virtual, but real both as lustful love and as a serious danger for her, for me, and for us. Prescriptively, the analytic guidelines for me were clear: Do not act; instead determine the context within which the emergent lustful desire arose and explore its present meaning and the influence of the past. How open or challenged I would be to following these guidelines would depend to a considerable degree on the answer to the component of the equation represented by the analyst's (my) love. Were I to have either fantasies or dreams and body arousal of lustful desire or responses of revulsion, contempt, or righteous indignation, I would have had to shift my focus from the patient to a self-regulatory introspection to contain myself within a professional stance. I would thereby lose my opportunity to enter a transitional space during which I could take her real lustful love and convert it momentarily into a virtual reality or reverie in which my knowledge of her past, her present, my past, and my present could open to erotic imagination held in balance by a spirit of inquiry (Lichtenberg, Lachmann, & Fosshage, 2002).

I can elaborate on the interplay between the analyst's and patient's contributions to transference love by using excerpts from the case of Sonya described in *Craft and Spirit* (Lichtenberg, 2005). Sonya began her treatment in a state of near-suicidal depression and total pessimism: "No one helps me. You will not help me. I went to an analyst for a year. I didn't talk, and he didn't talk. It was no help!" The first tiny inkling of a secure base of attachment love occurred about a month after beginning. Sonya came regularly (reassuring to me) and followed a ritual of not speaking spontaneously. I would ask, "How are you?" and she would answer, "Same." We would establish brief moments of eye and verbal contact by my tracking her as I would with an avoidant infant. One day, perhaps inspired by a slight change in her or a safe feeling for playfulness in me, I opened with "Same same?" Sonya responded with a flicker of a smile and a twinkle in her eye. I believe we had exchanged a moment of attachment love based on the secure base connection of our shared ironic humor.

In a later episode, Sonya (Lichtenberg, 2006) arrived exhausted with a terrible cold and insisted she would have to work late into the night. I commented on her conscientiousness, which we both valued, and the high quality of her professional work and the pride she derived from it, and I asked if it was necessary to deny her self-interest and physical needs to such a degree as she felt she had needed to in her family. Sonya's glare and stubborn silence told me my comments were to no avail, and we sat in a frustrated, ineffectual, disconnected silence. Responding to some slight movement on her part, I told her I was having a fantasy of picking her up, taking her home, putting her in bed, and bringing her some bouillon to drink (I remembered she was vegetarian, so chicken soup was out). After my venture into a virtual reality of demonstrable attachment love, Sonya said, "All right. I'll go home!"

At a moment when the waxing and waning of Sonya's depression had reached a dangerous downturn, I was determinedly trying to get her to consult with a neuropharmacologist to change her medication, and she was equally determinedly refusing. As we sat in yet another ineffectual silence, she caught a glance of helpless sadness on my face and asked, "What?" I responded, "You look like a sad little kitten." (The source of my remark and her particular response are described in detail in *Craft and Spirit*; Lichtenberg, 2006.) Sonya agreed to go, was greatly helped, and in a flurry of lively, even joyous, moments announced she had a surprise for me. She had developed a crush on a handsome Aussie tennis player and had arranged to go to his match and attend the team party after it. Romantic love had broken through, and I was its sponsor ("I have a surprise *for you*"). This emergence of romantic love was startling to both of us. Sonya had not dated even once since she was "dropped" by a man in graduate school (her father had left her mother for another woman). She regarded any interest from a man as only his desire to "hit" on her. At the tennis party, Sonia met a man she began to date and eventually married. My response to the opening of romantic love was comfortably in keeping with Sonya's transference placement of me as the pleased father–sponsor vicariously enjoying my patient–daughter's unfolding to a man. I did not sense myself experiencing jealousy or betrayal—that is, experiencing myself as involved in a triangular relationship. However, as I reflected on the timing and surprise of this entry of romantic love, I recalled a particular moment a month or so before when, despite her depressive state, I looked at Sonya as an attractive young woman, a man (I) could fall in love with. I have no idea what stirring in Sonya or in me triggered my thought/feeling at that moment, but I strongly believe that in the real and virtual intimacy of an analytic relationship how each carries the other in mind will affect the outcome both explicitly and implicitly.

Lustful love and its transgressive arousal states never entered into Sonya's analysis in any specific form, but attachment and romantic love appeared in a particular sequence of richly textured scenes. Some weeks after her first surprise, Sonya told me she had another surprise for me. She had gotten a kitten. Kitty provided Sonya with a playful companion and Sonya and I with a symbolic family. Sonya could establish an attachment love with her symbolic baby and our symbolic child, Kitty. I could coparent and enjoy Sonya's unambivalent good mothering attachment to Kitty. In the sessions or parts of sessions that Sonya devoted to Kitty's antics, our pairing took in a subtle, gentle romantic tinge, all while her dating relationship slowly deepened.

To conclude, I believe transference love in each of its forms—attachment, romantic, and lustful—must be real, must be genuine, and be experienced as authentic by both patient and analyst. For transference love to facilitate the therapeutic goal of analysis, attachment, romantic, and lustful love must be transferable into virtual reality. The imaginary transposition may be as concrete as my fantasy of feeding Sonya bouillon or as dreamlike as a romantic fantasy or a reverie about a child relieving his boredom by losing himself in masturbation. When inspired by a spirit of inquiry, words and images in their concrete, poetic, and metaphoric forms convey the linkage between the real and the virtual and imaginary.

CHAPTER 8

Coda

As I pull together the conceptual strands laid out about sensuality and sexuality, I as author, and you as reader, can consider the degree to which the book achieves my purpose, what is successfully included, what questions are unanswered, and what is omitted.

My purpose is both to offer a broad survey of the sensual–sexual motivational system and to present many detailed specifics that contribute to explicating my main themes. The broad survey lays out a developmental line from infant to adult based on the experiential distinction between sensuality described as body-centered, fantasy-elaborated pleasure and sexuality described as body-centered, fantasy-elaborated erotic arousal. In this conception, sensuality flows relatively nonconflictually between people, and sexual expression occupies a space that involves tension between behaviors previously or currently proscribed and practices that are sanctioned outlets. The detailed specifics that I present are drawn from such diverse areas as attachment research, infant research, clinically obtained case material, research on gender identity, research on strip club regulars, and body changes in puberty and during orgastic arousal. I am guided in my assessment of influences on sensuality and sexuality by my knowledge of traditional analytic recognition of psychosexual development; self-psychology; a relational, intersubjective, and family systems perspective; and cultural and sociological trends.

During my many presentations of these views, many excellent questions have been asked and criticisms leveled.

Does my presentation overstate the significance of sexuality or at least fail to place sensuality and sexuality in a balanced context with other motivational systems? Without my intending to give an unbalanced context portrayal, I accept that a reader could come to that conclusion. An entire book devoted to one motivational system gives that system considerable significance, which is as it should be. The same would be true if the book were about the psychic regulation of physiological requirements and the multitude of physiological dysregulated states. Or, a book could be focused on the aversive motivational system—the ability to handle controversy and to estimate and react to danger—and the myriad states of panic, rage, euphoria, depression, and shame. Or, a book could track the passage from an infant's exploration and assertion of preferences to an adult's pursuit of interests, efficacy, and competence in work and hobbies as well as disturbances in learning and blockages in utilization of intellectual and creative potential. I have placed the attachment–affiliative motivational system in context with the sensual–sexual system in many places in this book. However, the dynamic significance of continuous shifting of motivational dominance from system to system and within systems described in earlier books was largely outside the scope dealt with here.

Have I overemphasized the significance of shame? I believe this query has two parts. First, my claim that shame as an experience, and shaming as an interpersonal culturally determined enforcer of values by parents with their children are the determinants of a separate path for sensuality and sexuality, opens the question, Do sensuality and sexuality follow separate paths? A careful examination of the literature reveals a few comments that support my view of the separate paths, but none that I know give to it the significance that I do. So, my argument cannot be resolved by theory, although I believe my concept is both logical and coherent. My best support arises from the fit with experience. I strongly believe we experience the sensual pleasures our particular upbringing sanctions and affirms as a cherished unconflicted component of our attachment loving, one aspect of our romantic loving and, in analysis, one component of our bidirectional transference loving. The sensual components of our loving relations with self and others do not lead us to blush, to hide, to feel we have transgressed a boundary, or to feel we have subverted a personal or social value. Sensuality is vitalizing (or soothing). Sensual experience does not have the heightened arousal of orgasm or the blurring of boundaries. Sensuality does not combine exciting elements of power, possessiveness, and thrust and counterthrust. Sexuality, I claim, is all of what I have just said sensuality is not. Lustful love, whether a little girl or boy masturbating secretly under the covers, an adolescent girl or boy performing oral sex, or an adult lovemaking couple worrying that the walls of the hotel are too thin, has an edge, and that edge is itself a stimulus to the excitement. Having stated my justification based mainly on recognizable clear experiential factors, I must also agree that sensual and sexual experiences often do not have as definitive boundaries as the examples I use to support my proposal. The experiences, like most definable motivational experiences, have not only their edges but also their blends.

The second part of the question, Have I overemphasized shame? asks the following: Even if sensuality and sexuality are different experiences, is shame the main factor responsible for the divide? My claim is based on my belief that shame, or more properly shaming to induce shame and inhibit desire, is the major socializing force in body-centered pleasure seeking. Parents will induce fear to stop children from running out in the street or climbing up on chairs—and fear has been used to tell boys that playing with their penis will cause it to drop off. Fear of punishment inhibits, and receiving punishment and losing approval also shames. One person may label the feelings that inhibit her erotic desires as shame; another may label a similar or indistinguishable inhibiting feeling as guilt. An adolescent who as a child was made to feel his erotic desires directed at his mother were sinful may become so inhibited by his fear of a female's rejection and scorn that, with eyes down, he will avoid a girl's overtures. He may become sad at his loneliness, terribly ashamed of his cowardliness, and humiliated at the teasing of his friends. Shame can trigger anger or be the consequence of anger. Shame can be a component of depression and the sequel of a fear or panic state. How do we get out of this morass of affects? I could simply propose to add to my phrase "sensuality and sexuality across the divide of shame" the further qualifier "and shame-related affects (embarrassment, humiliation, and guilt)" or the broader qualifier "the divide of all negative affects." Freudian theory for the most ignored shame while privileging anxiety and guilt as the affects that inhibited, regulated, and socialized. Many contemporary students of shame have offered convincing evidence for the role of shame in the presymbolic toddler and oedipal periods during which the distinguishing pattern of what is approved and sensual and what is prohibited and sexual is established.

After a presentation of chapter 1, several members of the audience protested against my view of the inherent conflicted nature of sexuality. They argued that if the mother or parents presented their regulatory instruction, "Sammy, you mustn't do that," in a kindly empathic manner with helpful age-appropriate explanations, sensuality and sexuality could proceed seamlessly and joyously. Certainly, how prohibitions are presented affects the outcome (too timidly, no regulatory effect; too harshly, a potential traumatizing effect). However, a prohibition is a barrier, and the tension (conflict) that results from the attempt to overcome (transgress) its inhibiting effect can either lead to a joyous bodily and relational experience fueled by erotic imagination or to inhibitions or other disturbances of bodily expression and imagination as well as failed intimacy. But, looking within the family of the developing child or the particular lovemaking adult couple is not the context for assessing my core proposal. Rather than the "local level," the argument rests on a finding, however expressed, (e.g., incest taboo) that all cultures draw a line regarding which sensual pursuits are permissible and which are not. From culture to culture, the line drawn may be different, as may how strongly deviation is punished, but a line will be drawn, and deviation will be punished. The individual parents are the messengers of the cultural values, and the children are the beneficiaries or victims.

An opposite dissent states that the examples of parent–child interchanges I present are generally too tame. Consequently, I have failed to give an adequate tragic portrayal of the many families in which abusive practices (physical, emotional, or sexual) are commonplace. Although I mention many specific instances of sexual abuse, I do not present a lengthy discussion of the destruction of an adult sexual addictive perpetrator's sense of choice and worth and the stealing of a childhood from the victim conveyed by Nabokov in *Lolita*. I have regularly alluded to the more disturbing family responses to the whole area of child rearing, the responses to a child's needs for overall physiological regulation, attachment safety and intimacy, freedom to explore and assert preferences, and the management of aversive responses, as well as regulation in the sensual–sexual sphere. The key word in that defensive statement is *alluded*. My purpose has not been to emphasize pathology but to stay within the range of sensual and sexual issues that occupy what I regard as a broad middle ground of people and couples who could work out some strategy, whether stable and joyous or shaky and tension ridden, for their attachment and lustful love. Drawing on my clinical and own life experience, I can find little value in offering either a utopian or a predominantly pathological view of the basic developmental factors in humankind's pursuit of sensual and sexual desires.

Another criticism asks pointedly, Is what I have presented a psychoanalytic theory of sexual development? So much emphasis on sociocultural factors and on intersubjectivity devalues the intrapsychic dimension of conflict that for many is the sine qua non of an analytic theory. Moreover, I offer no mention of a sexual drive, of instinct, or of libidinal energy. Absent are familiar linguistic landmark references to repression and the dynamic unconscious; the repetition compulsion; the id, ego, and superego; defense mechanisms; internalization; and self and object representations. I have likewise for the most part omitted the use of self-psychological terms such as self-structure and selfobject. I have recast a core finding of Freud, the 4- to 6-year-old (oedipal) child's romantic love and rivalry to strengthen its utility as a fundamental developmental theory. Nonetheless, I recognize that I leave many readers without the comfort of familiar terms to orient their "psychoanalytic" thinking. My long familiarity with the terms of ego and self-psychology tells me that every time I would use the technical terms of these theories, I would drag along a lot of baggage I do not want. So, I try to incorporate the essence of the theories that I want to retain by conveying their meaning in more ordinary language, believing that the richness of understanding of human struggles, rather than technical terminology, is what determines whether a proposal is psychoanalytic.

Coming from the opposite direction, I have been asked if the persistent emphasis in the book on bodily experience constitutes a backdoor reentry of drive theory and a move away from a relational perspective. Particularly, the example in chapter 3 of research on the differences in predilections of male and female neonates and infants could be taken as giving biology predominance over intersubjective influences on gender identity. Historically, psychoanalytic theory has swung back and forth between valorizing either the body or the interpersonal aspects of development. Today, I believe most analysts regard the influence as bidirectional. I have placed the pendulum where my clinical and personal experience direct me with considerable humility regarding whether I have placed the emphasis optimally.

Finally, I come to my omissions, at least the ones I know. A reader perusing the table of contents will see Fathers and Daughters, Mothers and Daughters as the title of chapter 5 and wonder what happened to sons. My book is not a gendered tilted book or is not intended to be. The two longer case reports of Veronica (chapter 4) and Jane (chapter 6) are about females, but male case examples are plentiful throughout. The reason chapter 5 is skewed toward daughters is that the many advances in analytic understanding of female development have led to a new appraisal of parent–daughter relationships, which is what I have tried to capture. Throughout the book, whenever I describe female infants, children, adolescents, and adults and their intrafamily relationships, I believe I am viewing them from different eyes than my training led me to use. Building on my observations and those of others, I attempted to crystallize my perspective on female development using the paradigm of father–daughter and mother–daughter. I know of no comparable paradigmatic change in father–son or mother–son relationships and therefore have nothing on the same scale to add.

In a book designed to present a broad conception of sexuality, a reader might note the absence of any systematic discussion of homosexuality, and a limited discussion of gender identity, and I would agree apologetically with the reader. Our field is now blessed with a vast and informative literature on gay and lesbian development and sexuality and on the complexity of multiplicity in gender identity. I refer to a few of the authors of that literature from whom I have taken ideas explicitly. Others unmentioned by name have been sources for my reeducation. It is that revision in view that I have offered my reader. For much further conceptual richness on these subjects, I recommend the journal *Studies in Gender and Sexuality* and the work of its many contributors.

In a book in which I have emphasized the influence of cultural factors mediated through parents and peers, I have not presented a systematic account of the many changes in cultural attitudes and values that have and are occurring. A book for children written by a prize-winning author used the word *scrotum* to illustrate the puzzle children have with the meaning of words about the body. An outcry of "shamers" demanded the book be banned from schools and libraries; to many others, the issue of the word speaks to a puritanical absurdity. To most children, scrotum would seem too mild an expletive to use for transgressive fun. Along with my only touching here and there on cultural specifics, I have also not described the power of affiliative motives to remain true to a person's extended family of coreligionists, political tenets, race, and country of origin. Ultimately, all of these factors play out in the individual lives of each person and each couple trying to find the way to sensual and sexual fulfillment.

Last, I have offered little direct help to the practicing psychoanalyst or psychotherapist in treating the many patients with problems in sensuality and sexuality. I refer the reader to my recently completed *Craft and Spirit: A Guide to the Exploratory Psychotherapies* (Lichtenberg, 2006) for my clinical approach. I place my contribution in this book in the sequence of listening, understanding, and interpreting in an imaginary space between listening and understanding. I have often heard the advice to analysts to listen with a blank or open mind. I regard this admonition as both impossible and impractical. An analyst's listening is guided by a purpose: to explore the meaning of a communication with respect to what is influencing a patient in some aspect of his or her life that he or she hopes to gain help in managing better. To explore meaning requires knowledge of patterns of feelings, thinking, behaving, and relating and of expectations, intentions, inferences, and values in whichever area is under consideration. Knowledge of the patterns provides the background for sensitive, empathic, intelligent listening and comprehension of the themes of patient's inner lives, the patient's relationships with the cast of others brought on the analytic scene in the domain of their communications, and the patient's relationship ("real," fantasied, and enacted) with their participant listener analyst. My goal in the book is to offer knowledge of patterns dealing with explicit and implicit communications about sensuality and sexuality that are as close to human experiences as I can get. I advise you to take what you can from what I offer, give it a place in the back of your mind as you listen, and see if it increases your understanding of the themes you are attending. Hold my ideas in your understanding lightly, playfully, and flexibly. Be open to the possibility of biases and blind spots and track your premises based on the interchanges that follow.

References

Aktar, S. (2005). *The alphabet of psychoanalysis*. London: Karnac Press.

Altman, N. (2007). From fathering daughters to dottering father. *Psychoanalytic Inquiry.*

Ammaniti, M., Nicolais, G., & Speranza, A. M. (2007). Attachment and sexuality during adolescence: Interaction, integration or interference. In D. Diamond, S. Blatt, & J. Lichtenberg (Eds.), *Attachment and Sexuality.*

Amsterdam, B., & Levitt, M. (1980). Consciousness of self and painful self-consciousness. *The Psychoanalytic Study of the Child, 35,* 67–84.

Balsam, R. (2007). Fathers and the Bodily care of their infant daughters. *Psychoanalytic Inquiry.*

Benjamin, J. (1988). *Bonds of love*. New York: Patheon Books.

Bowlby, J. (1958). The nature of a child's tie to his mother. *International Journal of Psycho-Analysis, 39,* 350–373.

Brazelton, T. B., & Als, H. (1979). Four early stages in the development of mother–infant interaction. *The Psychoanalytic Study of the Child, 34,* 349–371.

Brooks, J., & Lewis, M. (1974). Infants responses to picture of self, mother and other. Princeton, NJ: Educational Testing Service, No. 100 (unpublished).

Buchheim, A., Kachele, H., and George, C. (2007). My dog is dying today: Attachment narratives and psychoanalytic interpretation of an initial interview. In D. Diamond, S. Blatt, & J. Lichtenberg (Eds.), *Attachment and sexuality.*

Cohler, B., & Galatzer-Levy, R. (2007). Freud, Anna and the problem of female sexuality. In D. Diamond, S. Blatt, & J. Lichtenberg (Eds.), *Attachment and sexuality.*

Corbett, K. (1993). The mystery of homosexuality. *Psychoanalytic Psychology, 10,* 345–357.

de Rougement, D. (1956). *Love in the Western world*. New York: Pantheon Books.

Dimen, M. (2003). *Sexuality, Intimacy, Power*. Hillsdale, NJ: The Analytic Press.

Dimen, M. (2005). Sexuality and suffering, or the Eew! factor. *Studies in Gender and Sexuality, 6,* 1–18.

Diamond, D., & Blatt, S. J. (2002). Prologue. In D. Diamond, S. Blatt, & J. Lichtenberg (Eds.), *Attachment and sexuality.*

Diamond, D., & Yeomans, F. (2007). Oedipal love and conflict in the transference/countertransference matrix: Its impact on attachment security and mentalization. In D. Diamond, S. Blatt, & J. Lichtenberg (Eds.), *Attachment and sexuality.*

Diamond, M. (2006). Masculinity unraveled: The roots of male gender identity and the shifting of male ego ideals throughout life. *Journal of the American Psychoanalytic Association, 54,* 1099–1130.

Eagle, M. (2007). Attachment and sexuality. In D. Diamond, S. Blatt, & J. Lichtenberg (Eds.), *Attachment and sexuality.*

Edelman, G. (1992). *Bright air, bright fire: On the matter of the mind*. New York: Basic Books.

Elise, D. (1997). Primary femininity, bisexuality, and the female ego ideal: A re-examination of female developmental theory. *Psychoanalysis Quarterly, 66,* 489–517.

Erikson, E. (1980). *Identity and the life cycle*. New York: Norton. (Original work published 1959)

Fast, I. (1979). Developments in gender identity: Gender differentiation in girls. *The International Journal of Psycho-Analysis, 60,* 443–453.

Ferguson, T., Stegge, H., & Damhuis, I. (1991). Children's understanding of guilt and shame. *Child Development, 62,* 827–839.

Fiedler, L. (1966). *Love and death in the American novel*. New York: Stein and Day.

Fivaz-Depeursinge, E., & Corboz-Warnevy, A. (1999). *The primary triangle: A developmental systems view of mothers, fathers, and infants. Basic Behavioral Science*. New York: Perseus.

Fonagy, P. (2001). *Attachment theory and psychoanalysis*. New York: Other Press.

Fonagy, P. (2006, January 27). *A genuinely developmental theory of sexual enjoyment and its implications for psychoanalytic technique*. Plenary address presented at the American Psychoanalytic Association meeting, New York.

Frank, K. (2005). Exploring the motivation and fantasies of strip club customers in relation to legal regulations. *Archives of Sexual Behavior, 34,* 487–504.

Freud, S. (1924). The dissolution of the Oedipus complex. *Standard Edition, 19,* 173–181. (Original work published in 1961)

Friedman, L. (2006). What is psychoanalysis? *Psychoanalytic Quarterly, 75,* 689–714.

Giddens, A. (1992). *The transformation of intimacy: Sexuality, love and eroticism in modern societies*. Stanford, CA: Stanford University Press.

Gilmore, K. (1998). Cloacal anxiety in female development. *Journal of the American Psychoanalytic Association, 46,* 443–470.

Glendinning, V. (1992). *Anthony Trollope.* New York: Knopf.

Goethe, W. (1774). *The Sorrows of Young Werther.* New York: Phaedra, 1967.

Goldberg, S., & Lewis, M. (1969). Play behavior in the year-old infant: Early sex differences. *Child Development, 40,* 21–31.

Green, A. (1996). Has sexuality anything to do with psychoanalysis? *International Journal of Psycho-Analysis, 76,* 871–883.

Greenson, R. (1968). Disidentifying from mother: Its specific importance for the boy. *International Journal of Psychoanalysis, 49,* 370–374.

Harlow, H. (1962). The heterosexual affectional system in monkeys. *American Psychology,* 17: 1–9.

Harris, A. (2000). Gender as a soft assembly: Tomboys' stories. *Studies in Gender and Sexuality, 1,* 223–250.

Harris, A. (2007). "Fathers" and "daughters." *Psychoanalytic Inquiry.*

Hartmann, H. (1958). *Ego psychology and the problem of adaptation.* New York: International Universities Press. (Original work published 1939)

Hesse, E., & Main, M. (1999). Second generation effects of unresolved trauma in nonmaltreating parents: Dissociated, frightening, and threatening parental behavior. *Psychoanalytic Inquiry, 19,* 481–540.

Herzog, J. (2001). *Father hunger.* Hillsdale, NJ: Analytic Press.

Holmes, J. (2002). Sense and sensuality: Hedonic intersubjectivity and the erotic imagination. In D. Diamond, S. Blatt, & J. Lichtenberg (Eds.), *Attachment and sexuality.*

Kernberg, O. (1995). *Love Relations: Pathology and Normality.* New Haven, CT: Yale University Press.

Kerner, I. (2004). *She Comes First.* New York: Harper Collins.

Kestenberg, J. (1956). Vicissitudes of female sexuality. *Journal of the American Psychoanalytic Association, 4,* 453–476.

Kiefer, C. (2007). From selfobjects to mutual recognition: Towards optimal responsiveness in father and daughter relationships. *Psychoanalytic Inquiry.*

Kleeman, J. (1975). Genital self-stimulation in infant and toddlers girls. In I. Marcus & J. Francis (Eds.), *Masturbation.* New York: International University Press.

Klitzing, K., Simons, H., & Burgin, D. (1999). Child development and early triadic relationships. *International Journal of Psycho-Analysis, 80,* 71–89.

Kohut, H. (1971). *The Analysis of the Self.* New York: International Universities Press.

Kohut, H. (1972). Thoughts on narcissism and narcissistic rage. *The Psychoanalytic Study of the Child, 27,* 360–400.

Kohut, H. (1977). *The Restoration of the Self.* New York: International Universities Press.

Korner, A. (1973). Sex differences in newborns with special reference to differences in the organization of oral behavior. *Journal of Child Psychology and Psychiatry, and Allied Disciplines, 14,* 19–29.

Korner, A. (1974). The effect of the infant's state, level of arousal, sex and auto-genetic stage of the caregiver. In M. Lewis & L. Rosenblum (Eds.), *The effect of the infant on its caregiver* (pp. 105–121). New York: Wiley.

Kulish, K (2006). Frida Kahlo and object choice: A daughter the rest of her life. *Psychoanalytic Inquiry, 26,* 7–31.

Kulish, N., & Holtzman, D. (1998). Persephone, the loss of virginity and the female Oedipus complex. *International Journal of Psycho-Analysis, 79,* 57–71.

Lachmann, F. (2000). *Transforming aggression.* Northvale, NJ: Aronson.

Lewis, M. (1992). *Shame: The exposed self.* New York: Free Press.

Lichtenberg, J. (1989). *Psychoanalysis and motivation.* Hillsdale, NJ: Analytic Press.

Lichtenberg, J. (2000). Hatred and its rewards: A case illustration. *Psychoanalytic Inquiry, 20,* 389–408.

Lichtenberg, J. (2002). Intimacy with the gendered self. *Selbstpsychologie, 7,* 40–60.

Lichtenberg, J. (2005). *Craft and Spirit: A Guide to the Exploratory Psycho-therapies.* Hillsdale, NJ: The Analytic Press.

Lichtenberg, J. (2006). *Craft and spirit: A guide to the exploratory psycho-therapies.* Hillsdale, NJ: Analytic Press.

Lichtenberg, J., Lachmann, F., and Fosshage, Jr. (1992). *Self and Motivational Systems.* Hillsdale, NJ: The Analytic Press.

Lichtenberg, J., Lachmann, F., & Fossage, J., (1996). *The clinical exchange.* Hillsdale, NJ: Analytic Press.

Lichtenberg, J., Lachmann, F., & Fosshage, Jr. (2002). *A Spirit of Inquiry: Communication in Psychoanalysis.* Hillsdale, NJ: The Analytic Press.

Lichtenberg, J., & Mears, R. (1996). The role of play in things human. *Psychoanalytic Psychotherapy, 13,* 3–16.

Lieberman, A., St. John, M., & Silverman, R. (2007). "Passionate attachments" and parental exploitations of dependency in infancy and early childhood. In D. Diamond, S. Blatt, & J. Lichtenberg (Eds.), *Attachment and sexuality.*

Main, M. (2000). The organized categories of infant child and adult attachment. *Journal of the American Psychoanalytic Association, 48,* 1055–1096.

Mayer, E. (1995). The phallic castration complex and primary femininity. *Journal of the American Psychoanalytic Association, 43,* 17–38.

Meares, R. (1983). *The metaphor of play.* Northvale, NJ: Aronson.

Meares, R., & Lichtenberg, J. (1995). The form of play in the shape and unity of self. *Contemporary Psychoanalysis, 31,* 47–64.

Messer, S., & Lewis, M. (1970). Social class and sex differences in the attachment and play behavior of the year-old infant. In S. Fisher (Ed.), *The female orgasm* (pp. 71–72). London: Lane, 1973.

Mikulincer, M., & Shaver, P. (2007). A behavioral systems perspective on the psychodynamics of attachment and sexuality. In D. Diamond, S. Blatt, & J. Lichtenberg (Eds.), *Attachment and sexuality.*

Mitchell, S. (2002). *Can love last? The fate of romance over time.* New York: Norton.

Morrison, A. (1989). *Shame: The underside of narcissism.* Hillsdale, NJ: Analytic Press.

Moss, H. (1967). Sex, age and state as determinants of mother-infant interaction. *Merrill Palmer Quarterly, 13,* 19–36.

Nabokov, V. (1955). *Lolita.* Paris: Vintage International.

Notman, M. (2006). Mothers and daughters as adults. *Psychoanalytic Inquiry, 26,* 137–153.

Offer, D. (1980). Adolescent development: A normative perspective. In S. I. Greenspan & G. H. Pollock (Eds.), *The course of life: Psychoanalytic contributions toward understanding personality development, Vol. 2, Latency, adolescence, and youth* (pp. 357–372). Washington, DC: National Institute of Mental Health.

Pavens, H. (1979). *The Development of Aggression in Early Childhood.* New York: Aronson.

Piaget, J. (1957). *Logic and psychology.* New York: Basic Books

Roiphe, H. (1968). On an early genital phase. *The Psychoanalytic Study of the Child, 23,* 348–365.

Roiphe, H., & Galenson, E. (1981). *Infantile origins of sexual identity.* New York International University Press.

Sears, R., Maccoby, E., & Levin, H. (1957). *Patterns of child rearing.* Evanston, IL: Row, Peterson.

Sherfey, M. (1966). The evolution and nature of female sexuality in relation to psychoanalytic theory. *Journal of the American Psychoanalytic Association, 14,* 28–128.

Smith, H. (2006). Love and other monsters: An introduction. *Psychoanalytic Quarterly, 75,* 685–688.

Spitz, R. (1962). Autoeroticism re-examined. *The Psychoanalytic Study of the Child, 17,* 283–315.

Sroufe, A., Egeland, B., & Carlson, E. (2005). *The development of the person.* New York: Guilford Press.

Stoller, R. (1975). *Perversion.* New York: Pantheon.

Tomkins, S. (1962). *Affect, Imagery, Consciousness, Vol. 1.* New York: Springer.

Tomkins, S. (1963). *Affect, Imagery, Consciousness, Vol. 2.* New York: Springer.

Tomkins, S. (1987). Shame. In D. Nathanson (Ed.), *The Many Faces of Shame* (pp 133–161). New York: Guilford Press.

Weinstein, L. (2007). When sexuality reaches beyond the pleasure principle: Attachment, repetition and infantile sexuality. In D. Diamond, S. Blatt, & J. Lichtenberg (Eds.), *Attachment and sexuality.*

Whipple, B., & Komisaruk, B. (1991). The G-spot, orgasm, and female ejaculation: are they related? In P. Kohari (Ed.), *Proceeding: First International Conference on Orgasm* (pp. 227–237). Bombay, India: VRP.

Young-Bruehl, E. (2007). On famous fathers and their youngest daughters. *Psychoanalytic Inquiry.*

INDEX

V

Veronica (patient)
  and Carlos, 70–72
  commentary, 80–82
  and Dick, 73–75
  and father, 90–91
  and Jerome, 68–70
  married and professional life,
    76–80
  and mother, 93–94
  presenting symptoms,
    67–68
Violence, sexual, 137